THE VANISHING AGE OF SAIL

W. Wood & Sons October
1833-
WILTON WOOD

THE VANISHING AGE OF SAIL

THE ILLUSTRATED JOURNALS OF KELSICK WOOD, SHIPBUILDER

SIMON FRANCIS BROWN

AMBERLEY

First published 2025

Amberley Publishing
The Hill, Stroud
Gloucestershire, GL5 4EP

www.amberley-books.com

British Library Cataloguing in Publication Data.

A catalogue record for this book is available from the British Library.

ISBN 978 1 3981 2491 2 (print)
ISBN 978 1 3981 2492 9 (ebook)

Typesetting by SJmagic DESIGN SERVICES, India.
Printed in Great Britain.

Appointed GPSR EU Representative:
Easy Access System Europe Oü, 16879218
Address: Mustamäe tee 50, 10621, Tallinn, Estonia
Contact Details: gpsr.requests@easproject.com, +358 40 500 3575

Contents

Introduction

At the heart of everything which follows lies a series of small notebooks, each no taller than a man's hand, their boards scruffy and nondescript. One is a muddy tan colour, another blood red, others darkened leather and one more a silvery grey. Several covers bear faint, encircled numbers in black ink. The little books have not been badly treated as such, but they have led full lives.

Their original owner was Kelsick Wood, a shipbuilder in Maryport, the small town on the Cumberland coast. Each volume is likely to have spent its days moving between Kelsick's coat pocket, his office at the shipyard and the family home opposite. Much of Kelsick's important business during the 1820s and 1830s was conducted in the inns and taverns of the town, and the journals may have joined him as he celebrated launches, discussed union trouble or supply problems with his fellow shipbuilders, or as he dined with current and future clients. London had its coffee houses but in Maryport the taverns reigned.

The journals contain everything one might expect. Kelsick notes down contracts for new vessels and then later their dimensions and construction details. He records the stock held in the timber yard and the coal consumed by the smithy. He writes out orders for sailcloth and calculates the likely cost of a cargo of timber. But this is only part of what their pages have to show us.

Kelsick was a man of surprises, with passions away from the shipyard. Nestled among the business of the yard are hundreds of illustrations. His artwork became more elaborate as the years passed. First a discreet doodle, then the occasional drawing of a vessel the yard had launched, and, increasingly as the 1830s grew older, anything and everything which came to mind.

Some of his pictures, such as the wonderful designs for figureheads, provide a window onto an ancient craft, but others are Kelsick's private record of the world around him, both real and imagined. In a life of responsibility, with clients, workers, a wife and children all making their demands, these pictures appear to have been painted for him and him alone. He drew humdrum objects, animals, birds, even fish and insects, but it is faces and figures that dominate. His bright and colourful

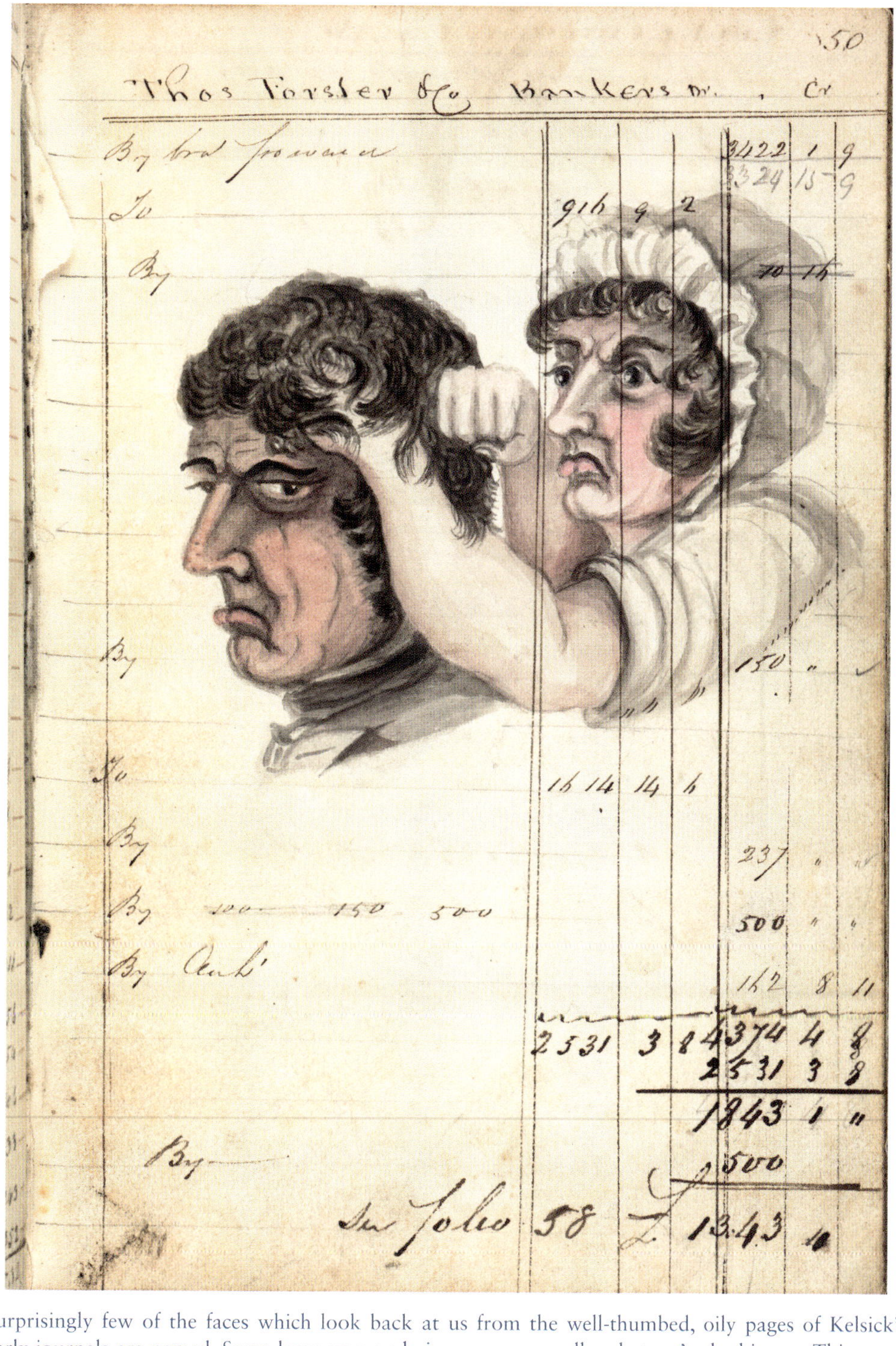

Surprisingly few of the faces which look back at us from the well-thumbed, oily pages of Kelsick's early journals are named. Some leave us wondering more generally what we're looking at. This scene is clearly domestic, but exactly what the man and woman are doing is not ours to know. There is a particular delight to be found in the informality of a private journal. Social conventions need not apply and the author can be as messy, lusty, angry or curious as he or she chooses.

pencil drawings and watercolours depict characters of all ages, races and walks of life. He had an eye for beauty but also for the grotesque, and alongside the faces of elegantly attired ladies and gentlemen, he painted others distorted in pain or anger.

The pages of earlier volumes are often specked with ink spots or greasy with thumbprints. Even the finest picture can double as a pad for a note on sail area or cordage requirements. These were working books, not intended to decorate the drawing room of a noble lady or to sit silently on the oak shelf of a galleried library. Volumes from later in the 1830s are more ordered, cleaner, and appear to have led a more sedentary life.

As the faces which look out from Kelsick's journals remind us, although these vessels were formed of timber, they carried the dreams and livelihoods of all those who owned, commanded and crewed them. The sea has always been a hostile place for man, and the fortunes of the masters and crews of these creaking wooden sailing ships were guided by skill, courage and chance. Some would meet violent, watery fates, while others would live out long lives, and observe from their retirement as the golden era of wooden-hulled sailing vessels faded slowly from view.

We are helped on our way by two other men of the town, each Kelsick's contemporary. Jonathan Douglas (1790–1838) was governor of the parish workhouse and an amateur poet. He acted as something of a roving reporter in 1830s Maryport, albeit a rather melancholy one. His collected poems were published in 1836. William Russell (1827–1907) was the son of a captain of one of the yard's vessels. He was still a child when Kelsick was running his shipyard, and he put his recollections to paper many years later. Together, these two men provide splashes of colour to help illuminate the little town, and Britain as a whole, at a pivotal point in its history.

The wooden brigs built at the yard have long since disappeared, but most of the journals from Kelsick's years in Maryport have survived. One found its way to the National Maritime Museum early in the twentieth century, but otherwise they have remained in just the manner they were created: closed to the world and private. Then, between 2017 and 2018, several of these little books appeared for sale with different dealers and auction houses, three volumes no more than a day's walk from the yard in Maryport. In the years since, art collectors, maritime historians and lovers of ephemera, marginalia or the unique and unusual have learnt of this little collection's existence.

Three volumes are in private hands at the time of writing, spanning the period between 1828 and 1837, and it is from these that the pages of this collection have been selected.

S. F. B.

Chapter 1
Origins

No wonder the sea not a moment can rest,
But tosses her waves to and fro,
And heaves, as with anguish, her troubled breast,
For the widows she's made, and the orphans oppressed,
And the tears she causes to flow.

'On the death of Alexander Ross,
who was drowned when bathing
in the sea' (extract)

The sea is never far from Jonathan Douglas's poetry. He presents it as beautiful but fickle, one moment wild, the next calm, an untameable force that shapes the lives of the little town's residents.

Britain's old shipyards were themselves boats on the ocean of the nineteenth century. Their fate would be determined in part by the course they set, by their skill and determination, but also by deeper currents running through a changing world.

First, we must get our bearings. Cumberland is among the most remote of England's counties, isolated by geography and set apart by history. All around it are barriers and boundaries. The Irish Sea lies to the west, and the imposing Cumbrian mountains rise in the east. To the north, the estuary waters of the Solway Firth declare the border with Scotland, and Hadrian's Wall stands nearby as the ancient marker between Roman Britannia and the wilds of unconquered Caledonia beyond. The region is one of the southernmost parts of our island where one can feel truly small in the face of the natural world.

The towns along the Cumbrian coast have long turned to the sea for their livelihoods. The Irish Sea provided convenient sailing routes to towns and cities all around its edges, from the west coast of England to Wales, Scotland, Ireland and the Isle of Man.

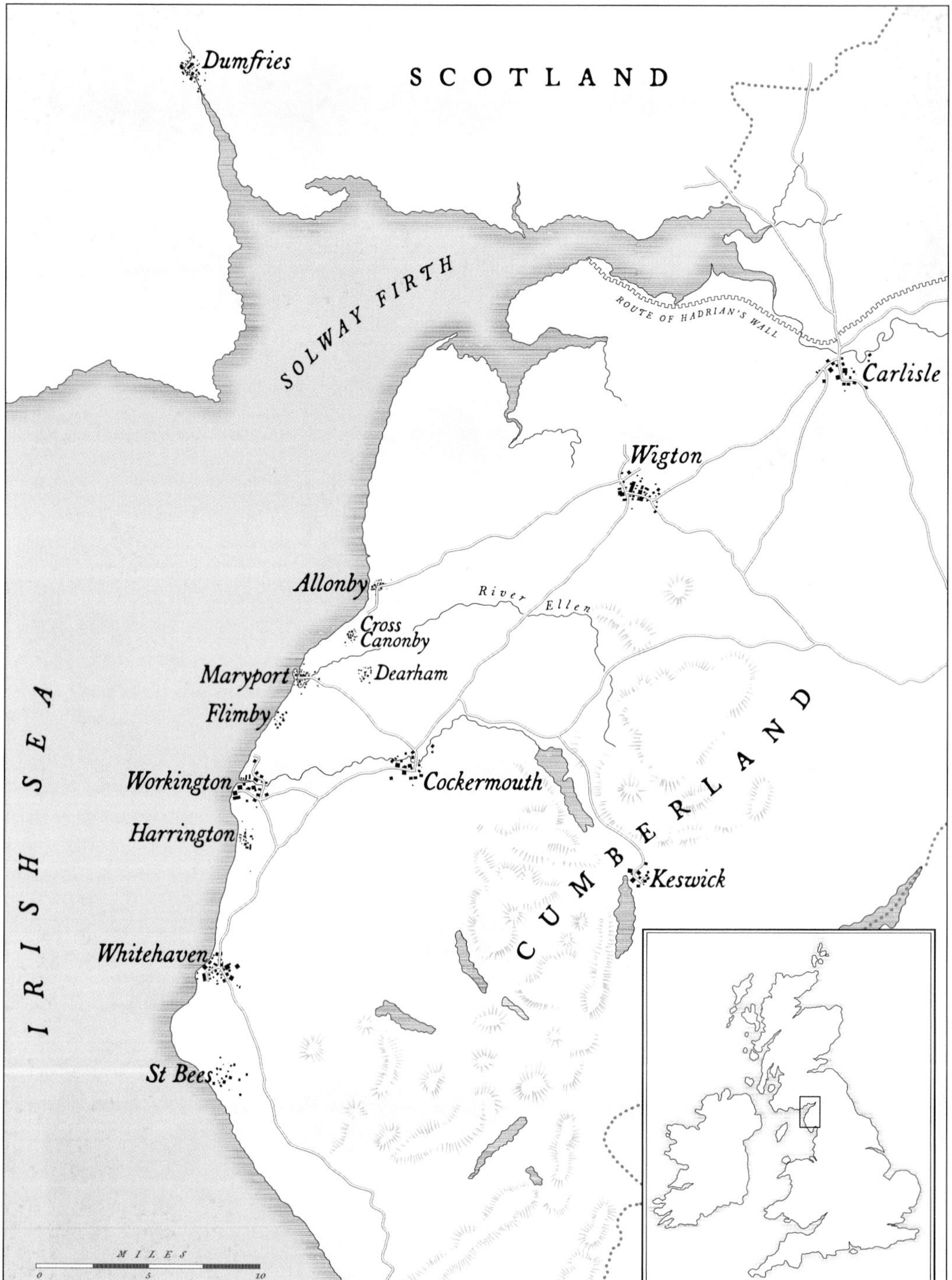

The historic county of Cumberland, based on *A Topographical Dictionary of England* (London, 1848). (All map artwork by David Atkinson, Hand Made Maps)

Buoyed by the nation's hunger for coal, Whitehaven and Workington established themselves among Britain's larger ports during the seventeenth and eighteenth centuries. Hundreds of small wooden sailing vessels travelled back and forth across the Irish Sea, delivering coal from the county's collieries to Dublin, Belfast, Dumfries and elsewhere.

Alongside the coastal traffic, larger vessels ventured further afield, into the Atlantic, to seek out commercial opportunities in the world beyond. Cumberland's ports could not rival London for volume, value or diversity, but Whitehaven in particular grew strong on the import of tobacco and later sugar.

And with shipping came shipbuilding. Myriad shipyards operated at towns along the coast, all competing to build the brigs, barques, schooners and doggers which kept Britain's national life and global mercantile success afloat.

Maryport lies along this coastline, at the mouth of the River Ellen, 27 miles to the south-west of Carlisle, and 6 miles north of Workington. At the time of Whitehaven and Workington's expansion, the inlet was home to a small hamlet called Ellenfoot. The site possessed little harbour infrastructure but was routinely used to load coal from local collieries onto flat-bottomed brigs which rested on its banks at low tide.

Ellenfoot's fortunes had changed in 1749 when Humphrey Senhouse, the wealthy local landowner, decided to exploit its potential more fully, reasoning that he could charge mine owners first for their coal to cross his estate and then further fees for the use of his harbour. His neighbours, the Lowthers of Whitehaven and Curwens of Workington, had seen great financial reward from similar investments. Senhouse obtained an Act of Parliament and set to work. He planned an enlarged harbour, designed a pattern of streets and named the nascent town in honour of his wife, Mary.[1]

Kelsick's uncle William Wood was among the first to arrive in the new town as Senhouse sought to bring businesses and jobs to his expensive venture. William established his shipbuilding yard on Strand Street and ran it with his nephew Thomas. Their first vessel was a brig named *Sally*, launched in 1765, barely a decade after the streets of the young town had been laid out.

Kelsick Wood, the man at the heart of our story, was born in Workington in 1771, the youngest child of Sarah Wilson and John Wood, William's brother and a shipbuilder in his own right. As a boy, the young Kelsick would have seen all manner of vessels arrive at Workington's harbour and depart for destinations around the United Kingdom and beyond. The livelihood of many of the town's inhabitants was connected to the water in some capacity, either directly as merchant mariner or fisherman, or through a related occupation such as shipwright or sailmaker. Among the more well-to-do were the merchants, shipowners and shipbuilders, such as the Wood family.

The final decades of the eighteenth century offered no shortage of topics for discussion at the Wood family dinner table. On the global stage, there was plenty to consider. In the year of Kelsick's birth, Captain James Cook returned to Britain aboard HMS *Endeavour* after his first circumnavigation of the globe, bringing

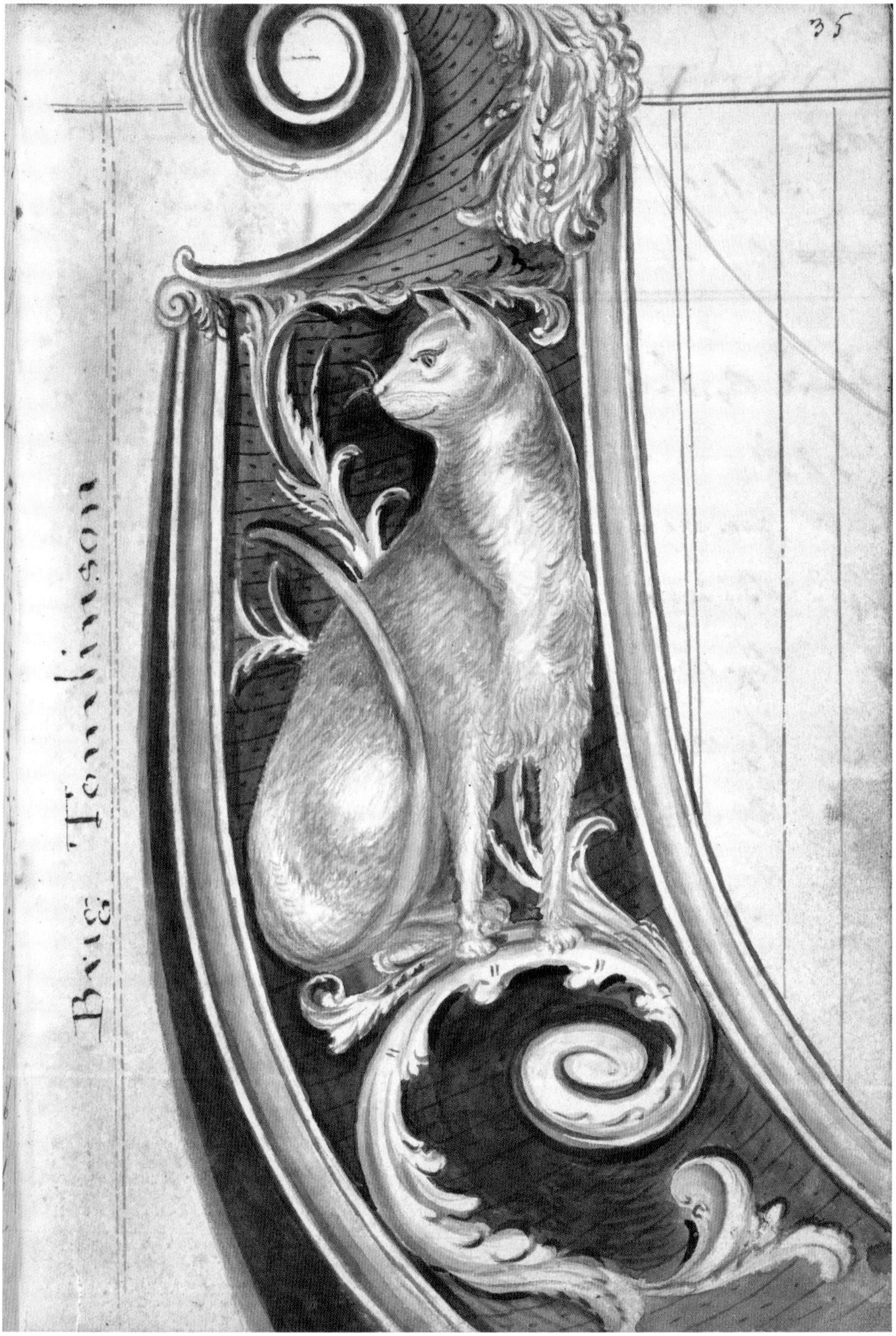

Not every vessel bore a figurehead. Many, like the *Tomlinson*, carried a more discreet carved billethead but used the space beneath it for further decoration.

reports of a great southern continent, before embarking on two more remarkable voyages of discovery. The American Revolutionary War continued through much of Kelsick's childhood, ending in defeat for Britain in 1783. Later that decade, as Kelsick turned eighteen in 1789, revolution swept through France as angry Parisians stormed the Bastille, followed by political turmoil, royal executions, and the increasing influence of a young general named Napoleon Bonaparte.

Closer to home, there was growing public and political debate about the horrors of the transatlantic slave trade and an increasingly prominent campaign for its abolition. Kelsick reveals his own views on slavery in his journals, at least those he held in the 1830s.

While Europe's monarchists observed the situation in France with growing concern, Britain was in the midst of a revolution of a different kind. The country was evolving from an agricultural to an industrial economy, and from a rural to an urban population, with all the social and cultural upheaval that entailed.

It was an era of scientific discovery and engineering innovation on a scale never before witnessed, and the north of England was at the heart of much of it. New techniques were emerging for both the extraction of raw materials and the production of manufactured goods. Mining efficiencies improved, helped by the advent of the steam pump to prevent deep mines from flooding and, by 1800, England was producing more iron and coal than the rest of the world combined. The increase in coal production gave the nation the source of cheap energy it needed to power its revolution.

The textile industry changed beyond all recognition. What had previously centred on a network of artisan, family enterprises became increasingly factory-based, with a lower-skilled workforce operating complex machinery on gruelling shift patterns. Production efficiencies and owners' profits grew dramatically, while working conditions deteriorated and industrial accidents increased. The rise of this dangerous, de-humanising machinery was met with direct resistance from some quarters. The Luddite movement, with its night-time break-ins and machine destruction, was at its most active in the 1810s, inspired by the legend of Ned Ludd, who was said to have destroyed two knitting frames in 1779.

Change came to different industries at different times, and shipping was one of the later endeavours to feel the effects of these repeated waves of innovation. The first steam-powered vessels emerged in the 1790s and 1800s, made possible by the improvements to the steam engine which James Watt had patented in 1769. Early models were inefficient and suitable only for use on canals and rivers, and later for coastal traffic, but several decades would pass before steam began to challenge the superiority of sail. Upon first seeing these noisy engines powering small craft over short distances, Kelsick's father and uncles may have found it hard to conceive that this dirty, unreliable technology might one day take business from the sailing ships which had dominated the world's oceans through the centuries.

Like many local boys, Kelsick's early years took him to sea. By 1793, still a young man of twenty-two, he was in command of the brig *Maria*, before moving four years later to the larger *Postlethwaite*. He traded primarily with Irish ports, with occasional voyages further afield to the Americas and the Baltic.

Perhaps to his wife's relief, Kelsick's years at sea ended in 1804, just after the short-lived Amiens peace treaty with France collapsed and the great navies of Europe prepared to face each other once more. A career in the merchant service could be as dangerous as one in the Royal Navy. Kelsick was sailing the same seas, vulnerable to many of the same threats and enemies, but without the comfort of a gun deck and red-jacketed marines to protect him.

He had married twice by this time. His first wife, Mary Nelson, had died after the birth of their son, John Nelson, in 1792, and Kelsick had remarried four years later.

Kelsick and his second wife, Mary Inman, had nine children together between 1799 and 1812. Tragedy came early to the couple, though, as disease and other hazards took their familiar toll. Two Sarahs and a Thomas died in infancy, while a first John and then James each perished before their eighth birthdays. Two other children, Agnes and Wilton, would reach adulthood but die before turning thirty. By the end of 1832, just three of Kelsick's ten children remained: John Nelson, John and Kelsick Junior. No parent should have to bury their child but, for many families in Georgian England, it was the norm.

The family settled into domestic life in Carlisle, where Kelsick, in need of employment, ran his brother-in-law's hat factory. It was an unlikely and short-lived career change. Five years later, Kelsick and Mary relocated once more, to take over the shipyard in Workington, once managed by his father John and more recently his brother Wilton.

Kelsick's shipbuilding interests became increasingly diverse in the decade that followed. He had entered an early partnership with his nephew Adam, who ran a shipyard and timber business in Maryport, but retired from this not long after moving to Workington. Other partnerships followed. Kelsick brought Thomas Peile into the Workington yard as partner and entered a similar arrangement along the coast in Harrington. A further opportunity presented itself in 1817, when Adam put the yard in Maryport up for sale. With the help of another partnership, this time including his eldest son, John Nelson, Kelsick added Maryport once more to his portfolio.

Each new partnership meant dealing with a further group of partners, which brought its own frustrations. Among a collection of family letters at the Carlisle Archive is one from an unhappy Kelsick, dated about 1819. He grumbles about his many partners' 'different tempers and dispositions', and complains that the business conducted at their private meetings then becomes 'the quay and tea-table talk for weeks afterwards'.[2]

Such ambitious expansion also left Kelsick dependent on an upturn in the country's volatile economic situation, and an end to the bad harvests which had blighted the last few years. The same volume of letters shows his young son Wilton writing to his mother with nervous optimism in January 1821: 'I trust that (the) Maryport concern will do great things for us all. For you know, trade

This page gives the particulars of vessel No. 30, the *Tomlinson*, launched by the yard in January 1835, two years before Queen Victoria ascended to the throne. The picture at the centre shows Britannia, the national personification of Britain, with spear in one hand and a crown-topped Union shield in the other. The anchor at her feet is a symbol of maritime dominance, and the rather small and tired-looking lion is intended to show the nation's strength and power. Kelsick rarely portrays women fully topless but often, as here, allows a dress or shawl to slip coyly from a shoulder.

33

Prime cost Teak by the Sylla

1835 August 20

Laurie Hamilton & Co

91 loads 22 ft @ 52/6 — 240. 0. 7

43 loads 10 ft @ 47/6 — 102. 12.

15 loads 22 @ 26/3 — 20 5. 3

362. 17. 10

150 – 4

Freight of do 150 loads

134 loads 39 ft above 20 ft @ 4.10 – 606. 10. 2

15. & 22 – under 20 ft @ 3. – 46. 6. 5

652. 16. 7

5. 0. 0

25. 0. 0

75. 0. 0

£1121. 0 –

7118 ft

£1121. – one foot

This page records the yard's purchase of teak from merchants Laurie, Hamilton & Co, delivered by the *Sylla* on her return from Sierra Leone in August 1835. The sexing of ships is a long-standing topic for debate. In a book so firmly anchored in the Georgian era, named vessels are feminine. Masters and crews spoke of them as such.

is often sick but never dies, according to an old merchant here who knows my brother.'

Shipyards are complex and expensive enterprises. With Kelsick still in Workington, it fell initially to John Nelson to provide the close management the Maryport yard required. In the early 1820s, however, Kelsick extricated himself from his other commitments. He dissolved the Maryport partnership, freeing John Nelson to pursue other interests in Liverpool, and prepared to take personal control of the yard. He relocated to Maryport and lent his name to the business, from which time it was known as Kelsick Wood & Sons, with Kelsick now entrusted to safeguard the family's shipbuilding fortunes.

Chapter 2
Around the Yard

How smiling, soothing, and serene
Is nature clad in sober grey;
And lovelier far the evening scene,
Than all the blaze of busy day,
When toil and tumult never cease,
And pleasure's always mixed with pain.

'The Setting Sun' (extract)

Kelsick Wood and Jonathan Douglas were men cut from different cloth. Kelsick emerges from records as an outgoing character, a man at the centre of the town's affairs, drawn to company and forging ties with his clients, family and community.

Jonathan appears as rather a solitary figure. He may simply have been channelling Wordsworth, wand'ring lonely as a cloud, but whenever opportunity presented itself, Jonathan left the bustle of the town behind. He escaped to the beach, the fields or the hills, anywhere he could quietly reflect on the natural world and the human condition. Not for him the busy day, 'where toil and tumult never cease'.

Kelsick, by contrast, appears to have thrived on it.

Kelsick's shipyard occupied a prime site at the mouth of the River Ellen. On one side, the long North Pier extended into the water, while to the south, a shorter, stubbier pier known as the Tongue partitioned the shipyard's waterfront from the wider harbour. The enclosed area was known for a time as New Harbour, always a dangerous naming strategy in a fast-changing environment. For the last 150 years, it has been North Harbour, and that is what we will call it here.

Behind the shipyard was an area just large enough for three narrow streets. Strand Street lay closest to the shore, then King Street and Nelson Street to the rear. Camp Hill rose sharply behind, interrupted by Brow Street, which ran diagonally up the steep incline. Together, the barriers of the river, sea and imposing cliff line created

Two men and a bird share this page with purchases of elm and coal tar from January 1831. Kelsick's gentlemen are in a dispute which seems to have descended into name-calling. Faced with the agitated man in green on the left, the man in the blue jacket simply sticks out his tongue.

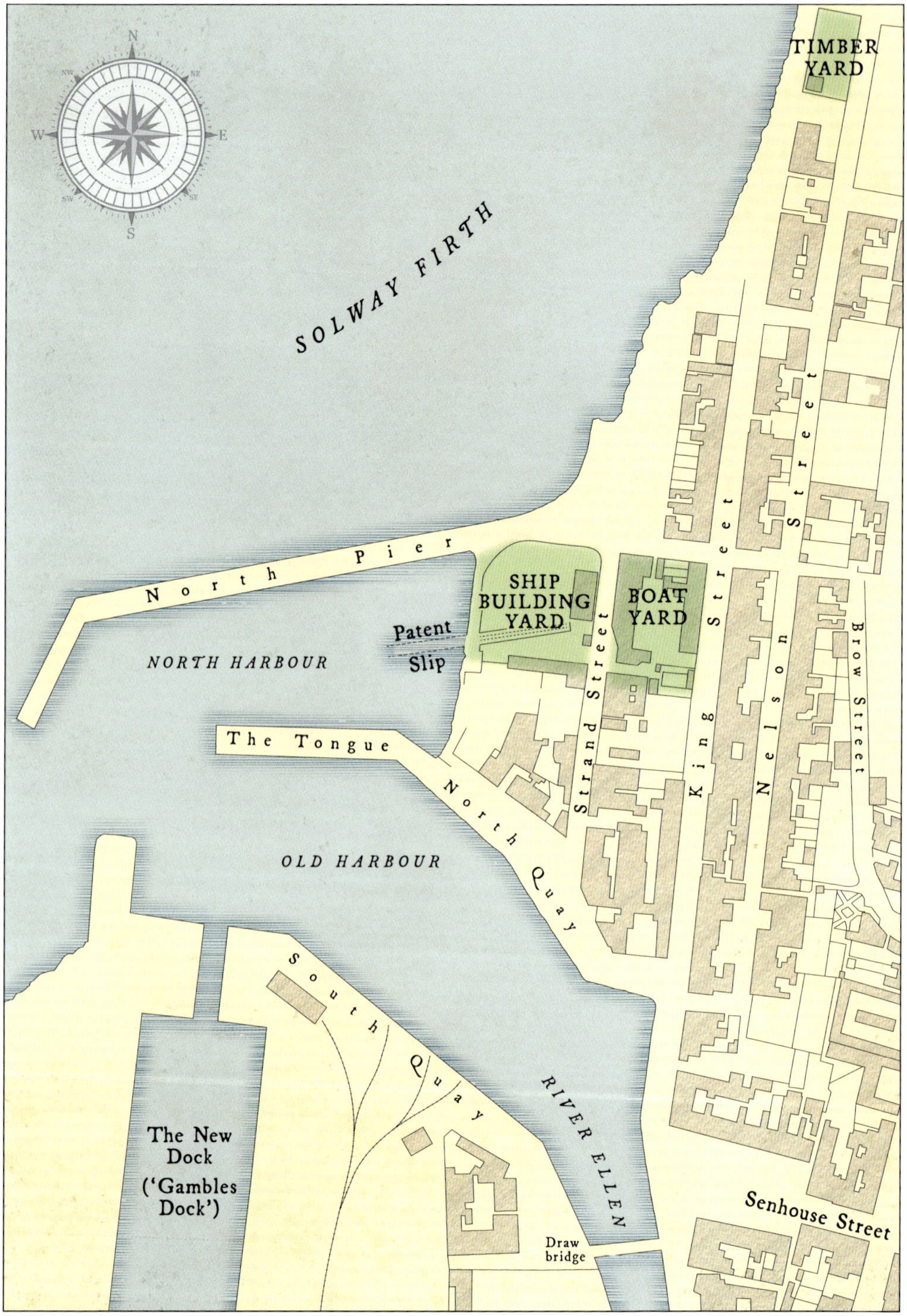

This map of Maryport harbour is based on one by W. Mitchell, dated 1834 and 'most respectfully inscribed to the Lord of the Manor, Humphrey Senhouse, Esq.'.

a distinct community at the foot of the town. The area was known traditionally as Down Street, although no such street existed.

North Harbour provided Kelsick's shipwrights with barely 50 yards of waterfront, but the business extended inland into three areas, all together making a site of about an acre.

The shipbuilding yard behind the water's edge occupied an area of nearly 2,000 square yards and included a moulding room, saw-pits, offices and assorted sheds, as well as a newly installed iron railway track, or 'patent slip', with a capstan at its rear.

On the opposite side of Strand Street, close to the Wood family home, lay the boat yard, home to the smithy, the rigging loft, the rope house and other buildings. Together with the workers' terraced houses which surrounded it, this added a further 2,000 square yards. The last part was the all-important timber yard, another 700 square yards, located a short walk away at the end of King Street.[1]

The town of Maryport had expanded considerably in the years since William Wood had established his business, but the scale of the shipyard's activities had changed but little. The yard could never be a large operation, its share of North Harbour and the restricted space inland would not allow it. It was distinctly small when compared with the Royal Dockyards or those of the East India Company, but the area was spacious enough for the projects which the family took on. Within this tight space, the yard produced between two and three merchant vessels each year, with a typical capacity of between 100 and 300 tons burthen.

THE *PARAGON* (1835): BUILDING A MERCHANT BRIG

The first mention Kelsick makes of the *Paragon* is a brief note dated 5 August 1834, to record that, 'This day contracted with Mr Dawson of Whitehaven to build a new vessel', followed by a summary of dimensions and cost. The *Paragon* is one of the best-documented vessels in Kelsick's journals, with rough notes and neater records spread among their pages, and she makes a good choice from which to explore the wider business.

George Dawson was a merchant who had formerly lived in Antigua and was now an established figure within the Whitehaven sugar market. The *Paragon* would be the first vessel on which Kelsick and Dawson had worked together.

By 1834, Kelsick's reputation as a master shipbuilder was well established. He would have cut an imposing figure. A wooden bust now in a Delaware museum shows him as a large man, stocky-framed and with a strong nose and prize-fighter's chin. His hair may be thinning, but his thick-set neck and broad shoulders look ready to carry the weight of the family business and indeed the whole town upon them.[2]

It was common for a prospective client like Dawson to receive a tour of the yard. It allowed the client to inspect whichever build was underway and let Kelsick showcase the fine workmanship of his carpenters. Nothing sold the yard's talents better than the sight of a fine new brig nearing completion on the stocks. Kelsick and client could then continue their discussion of the particulars over lunch, at the Golden Lion perhaps, a short walk away on Senhouse Street.

Dawson was commissioning his new vessel with a clear purpose in mind, to transport barrels of unrefined sugar, molasses and rum from his warehouses in Antigua to the market in Whitehaven. The two men settled on her dimensions: the vessel was to be a brig, with an 86-foot keel length, a beam width of 23 feet and a draft of 15 feet, giving her an estimated cargo capacity of 203 tons burthen when loaded to a proper sea trim. The costing of a project was commonly done on a per-ton basis. Assuming Dawson wanted his vessel fully fitted out, Kelsick noted that it would be priced at £15 5*s*. per ton. She was to be named the *Paragon*.

Kelsick and Dawson also settled upon the schedule of payments: four instalments, each of about £773, payable at significant points during the construction. As Kelsick carefully recorded in his small, red journal, the first would be due at the laying of the keel, the second after the full frame was in place, the next when the hull had been fully planked, and the final instalment was to be paid when the new vessel was launched and fitted out. The total cost to Dawson would be £3,095 15*s*.

With the contract signed, Kelsick's craftsmen could plan the construction of the vessel in more detail. The project would take many months from commission to delivery and would involve harnessing the yard's collective skill and experience, an intricate dance between craftsmanship, precision and logistics, with lots of sawing and hammering.

Kelsick's years in Maryport spanned the final decades of the Georgian era and the beginning of Victoria's long reign. Shipbuilding had been relatively untouched by the upheaval of the Industrial Revolution to this point. The yard's workers were traditionally skilled craftsmen using hand tools to turn timber, hemp rope and canvas into ocean-going sailing ships. Even many of the nails were wooden.

For all of the insight that Kelsick's journals give us, questions remain about the typical design habits of small merchant shipyards, as a notable lack of plans survive from this era. Much of the historical record of shipbuilding in Georgian Britain relates to the practices of the Royal Dockyards, where naval architects worked on expensive men-of-war and where draughtsmen produced intricate, geometrically precise plans in sheer, half-breadth and body view.

For a smaller, provincial yard like Kelsick's, we are left to debate the extent to which planning and design steps would have been started afresh for each new vessel, and how far the project would have relied on centuries of accumulated experience.

Contemporary handbooks inevitably break the processes down to their most formal and theoretical underpinnings. The *Shipwright's Vade-Mecum* (1805) places arithmetic and geometry at the heart of every young shipwright's education. It is reminiscent of the algebra and trigonometry that a young midshipman was expected to master.

The first sections deal with theory, everything from vulgar fractions and duodecimals to the extraction of the square root and cube root. Next comes an equally intense section on geometric theorems. These concepts are not presented entirely in the abstract. The handbook describes how to apply them either in the shipyard or at sea and how to use a slide rule to perform calculations. There are

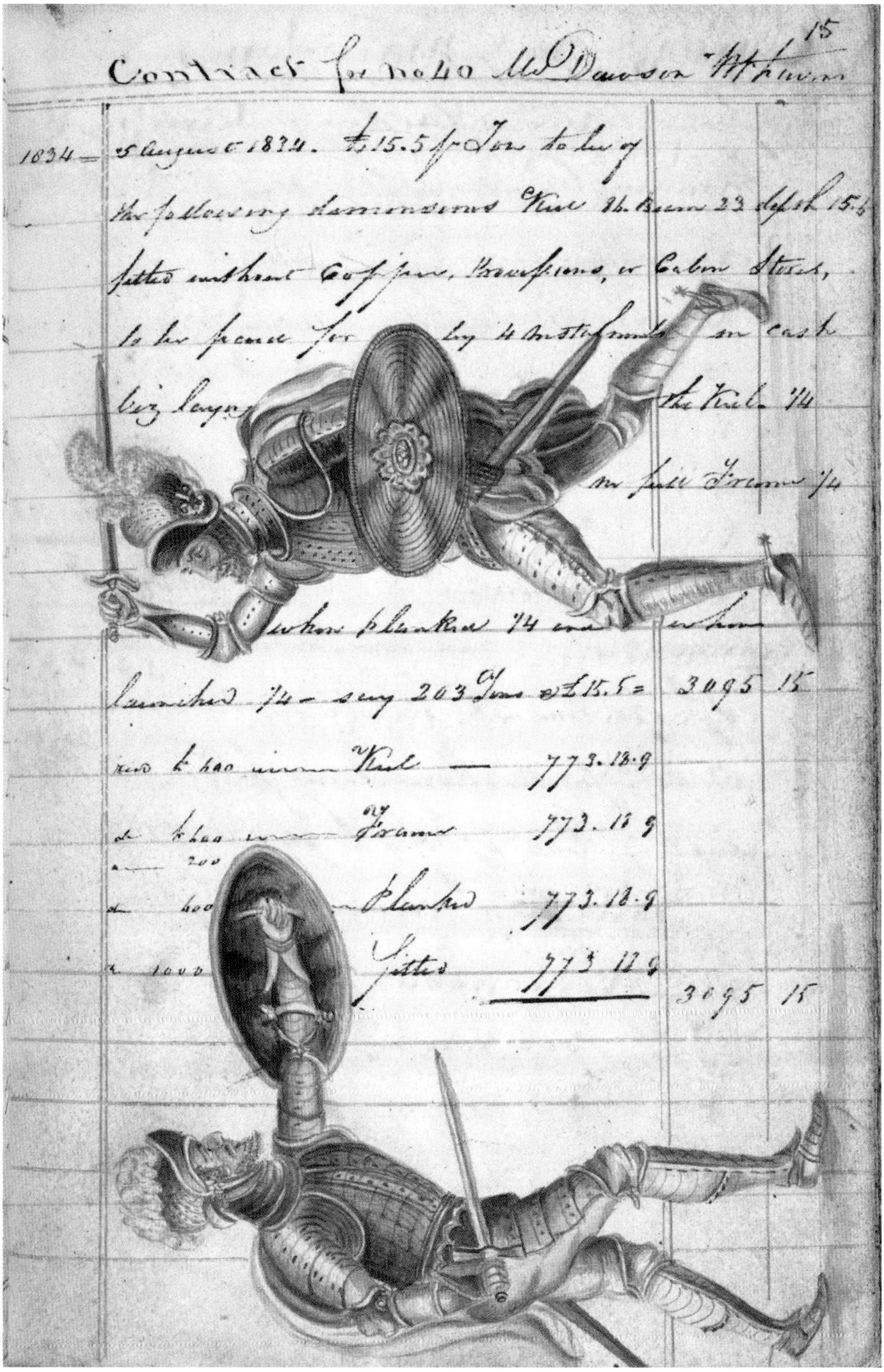

15
Contract for No 40 Mr Dawson
1834 — 5 August 1834. £15.5 per Ton to be of
the following dimensions Keel 84 Beam 23 depth 15.6
fitted without Copper, Provisions, or Cabin Stores,
to be paid for by 4 instalments in cash
viz ... the Keel 74
... full Frame 74
when planked 74 ... when
launched 74 — say 203 Tons @ £15.5 = 3095 15
... Keel — 773.18.9
... Frame 773.18.9
... Planked 773.18.9
... fitted 773.18.9
3095 15

The two knights in armour battling their way across the page share their arena with the costs and payment profile for George Dawson's vessel, the *Paragon*. Kelsick numbered each vessel the yard produced; a wise move given the tendency of owners to change their new vessel's name at the point of registration. The *Paragon* would be No. 40. Unfortunately, Kelsick is not always consistent in numbering between his lists. Elsewhere, the *Paragon* appears as No. 41.

also methods for transferring the lines of a plan to their true dimensions on the moulding loft floor, calculating a ship's tons burthen and finding its centre of gravity.

'Tons burthen' is a term worth explaining at the outset. Until 1849, when the rise of steamships forced a rethink, a ship's tonnage was calculated using Builder's Old Measurement, a calculation based on the vessel's length and maximum beam or width.

$$\text{Tonnage} = \frac{(\text{Length} - (\text{Beam} \times \frac{3}{5})) \times \text{Beam} \times \frac{\text{Beam}}{2}}{94}$$

Alan Forsyth, in his book *Highway to the World,* takes a more pragmatic view of a small yard's working habits and suggests that very few of these brigs were 'designed' in the way that larger and later vessels were. A typical Cumbrian brig was built for strength and durability rather than speed, and yard workers were already familiar with the scale and design of the vessels they were building. A small half-model might be prepared while the lines of the hull were being finalised with the client, built up from thin layers of wood bolted together, which could then be disassembled and scaled up to give a true set of dimensions.

The next part of the process took place in the moulding loft, which at Kelsick Wood & Sons was attached to the shipbuilding yard. Moulds were full-sized templates fashioned from thin wooden strips, for use by the sawyers and shipwrights to ensure that timber of the right dimensions would be selected and each length cut correctly to size. With the necessary measurements, moulds and timber specifications in place, construction could begin.

TIMBER

Central to the success of every shipbuilding business was a well-stocked and well-managed timber yard. The wood which the yard required arrived at Maryport by sea, some sourced from within the British Isles but most imported from further afield. Britain's native resources had been heavily depleted over the centuries, whereas timber from the forests of North America and the Baltic was still plentiful.

Once unloaded, each piece had to be carried or carted to the timber yard at the end of King Street, beyond the Quaker's meeting house and burial ground. As an added complexity, it then had to be left to season, often for a year or longer, sheltered from the elements but exposed to the air. Unseasoned or 'green' timber was certainly softer and easier to work with but was liable to distort as it aged. The consequence for a ship at sea could be catastrophic.

It was not in the yard's interest to cut corners in its choice of timber. Although principal clients might be from out of town, with their business interests in Liverpool, Whitehaven or Workington, minority shareholders often included friends, even family, and the yard's vessels were regularly commanded and crewed by local men. The wood had to be of sufficient quality to meet the rigours of the world's oceans, to bear the weight of a heavy cargo and to deliver its master and crew home safely.

With its exaggerated mane and unnatural pose, this lion is heraldic, *passant guardant*, full face and with right forepaw raised, the same lion that has appeared on the coat of arms of England since the twelfth century. Several actual lions were touring England with the caravans of Wombwell's Menagerie during the 1830s (including one named Wallace who would later swallow Albert Ramsbottom whole in Marriott Edgar's children's poem 'The Lion and Albert').

Kelsick's selection of woods for the *Paragon* included British and American oak, elm, pine and iroko. Each species behaved differently in response to the stresses to be applied to it, whether submerged in water or exposed to air. Beyond these material properties, cost and availability had also to be considered. The shipwright's understanding of each wood's qualities, and his ability to select the right piece of timber for the job, would be a major factor in the success of the vessel being constructed.

A CARGO OF AFRICAN TEAK

Kelsick's heraldic lion is surrounded by his continued calculations for a cargo of African teak from Laurie, Hamilton & Co., to be delivered by the *Johns*. African teak, or iroko, was an attractive, dense, durable hardwood, with natural oils to protect it from decay, but it was also expensive. The company have quoted Kelsick for five different lengths, ranging downwards from a top price of £45 per load for timber over 23 feet (a load being 50 cubic feet).

Unfortunately for Kelsick, less than one-third of the total cost will be for the wood itself. For each £45 load of the longest lengths, he will pay an additional £87 6*s*. in freight charges, £10 in duty, £4 2*s*. in insurance and a further £1 4*s*. in expenses. Timber with a list price of £45 will cost him £148 2*s*.

Kelsick applies these costs per load to his projections and works through his assumptions. The *Johns* will bring him (say) 190 loads, so 9,500 cubic feet in total, a volume roughly equivalent to three London double-decker buses.

There is another factor he must consider. Unless the timber has been squared off, gaps will remain between the circular logs once loaded onto the *Johns*. This is lost space, but he will be charged just the same. The sides of squared-off timber could be measured by mechanical calliper, but string was typically used to determine the circumference of circular logs. Kelsick reduces what he expects to receive by roughly 7 per cent to 8,820 cubic feet, string measure. Purchasing timber was a slow and costly business.

If needed, Kelsick could turn to his journals to justify the use of this exotic hardwood to his clients. In September 1831, he invited a group of gents to the yard to witness an experiment into the relative merits of British oak and African teak. Kelsick documented the two parts of his test with all the earnestness of a well-taught schoolboy. He weighed identical cubes of each wood and then compared the strength of 4-foot lengths by suspending increasingly heavy weights below. Kelsick announced his conclusion with equal clarity: African teak was both slightly lighter and significantly stronger than British oak.

THE SHIPBUILDING YARD

Once the timber had been selected, the job of the sawyer was to turn it into the planks or beams required. Before the rise of mechanised sawing machines, this was done by a pair of sawyers working in unison in a saw-pit. Each log was positioned over a deep hole in the ground. The more experienced sawyer stood atop and guided the saw's teeth, while a junior sawyer or an apprentice such as Daniel Maggot or George Bell added muscle from the dark, dusty pit below. The yard ran on the energy of these young apprentices, learning a trade in return for a small income. Kelsick's journals name his tenants and apprentices with reliable regularity, but rarely his employees.

Attention now shifted to the shipwrights, or ship's carpenters. The lines of seafaring vessels had evolved through the centuries but much of the shipwright's craft had remained unchanged. Before construction could begin, heavy wooden keel blocks were positioned on the firm, flat ground behind North Harbour, tall enough to allow men to work on the hull which would soon rise above. The line of keel blocks grew progressively shorter as they approached the water, creating the incline which would ensure that the vessel would not be left immovable and landlocked.

The first part of the *Paragon* to be laid down would be the thick and sturdy timbers of the keel, which acted as the ship's backbone and around which the rest of the hull would be constructed. Once the sections had been scarphed to form a single rigid length, shipwrights could attach the stem, which shaped the bow of the vessel, and the sternpost, from which the rudder would later be hung.

Skipping with such brevity through the hull's construction risks reducing it to a set of modern flat-pack instructions. The process was intricate and involved, and the carpenter's technique the result of centuries of refinement. It came with a technical language all of its own, a world of futtocks, strakes and transoms, ribbands and harpins, rabbets and coaks. For more detail than would be appropriate here, John Fincham's *An Introductory Outline of the Practice of Ship-Building &c. &c* (1821) was written as a primer for students at the School of Naval Architecture in Portsmouth. It gives an accessible, even patient, account of the complex process, although the steady layering of technical terms can quickly overwhelm a mind which wanders even for a moment.

As the build began to rise above the keel blocks, shipwrights erected scaffolding and platforms to permit the many different workers access to all parts of the hull. Timber A-frames allowed for the lifting of heavy pieces into place.

With her contract signed in August and her launch the following May, the *Paragon* was a winter build. November and December of 1834 were unseasonably warm and 'delightfully mild', but that all changed in the New Year. The weight and width of North Pier kept the powerful winter waves at bay but the shipwrights in the yard behind it were exposed to the elements. January 1835 brought frost and snow, and February was little better. The grey skies were often heavy with rain, the wind cold and raw. The North Atlantic might bring squally showers or torrential day-long downpours but if no one worked, the yard could not function.

Next came the oak ribs, or frames, fastened together using wooden dowels, known as treenails or trunnels. Shipwrights secured each frame to the keel, and then laid the keelson above, helping to secure the heavy frames in position. Transverse beams were added to unite the port and starboard frames, with sturdy knees to strengthen the structure further. The framework of the new vessel was now secure, its form reminiscent of the upturned skeleton of an immense whale, its sun-bleached bones lying unseen on a distant Arctic shore.

The accuracy of the shipwright's earlier work on the vessel's frame would now be put to the test, with the laying of the decks and planking of the exterior. To ensure the long oak planks would lay flat against the curves of the *Paragon*'s hull, each was softened, typically in a steamchest. The inner planking followed, which added strength and lined the interior of the cargo hold.

Among the wood laid down in the timber yard were the long straight lengths of pine or fir which would be fashioned into the *Paragon*'s masts, yards and spars. The sawyers first squared off the logs, before shipwrights set to work to remove excess wood along the lengths until the outline of the circular sections of mast slowly appeared above a bed of wood chippings.

The shipwrights working on the hull gave way to the caulkers, who arrived with their caulking irons, mallets and oakum, a mixture of tar and old rope fibres. The caulkers worked their way through the hull, driving strands of oakum into every seam and sealing them with hot tar to ensure the structure would be watertight.

Caulking required hemp fibres and the tar with which to mix it. In the eighteenth century, this had been exclusively wood tar, known as 'stockholm tar' because of the near monopoly held by the Scandinavian states. In the industrial spirit of the times, however, engineers patented processes for extracting tar from coal. Kelsick's records show orders for both types.

It was not enough simply to waterproof the *Paragon*'s wooden hull; it also had to be protected. The outer planking was first coated in pitch below the waterline and then sheathed in copper sheeting to deter the teredo mollusc or 'shipworm', which would happily bore into timber at an alarming rate, faster in the world's warmer seas.

These were not permanent solutions, however. Caulking would need to be repeated regularly during the life of Dawson's vessel as the continual stresses of the Atlantic weather and waves caused fresh gaps to emerge. Similarly, the copper sheeting would slow but not eliminate the problem of fouling, and barnacles, seaweed and sludge would continue to accumulate below the waterline, increasing drag as the vessel moved through the water.

In the painting of the launch of the *Collingwood*, seen later in this book, the new-built brig is about to be launched above the tracks of the patent slip on the southern side of the yard's waterfront, but the principal function of this little iron railway was the reverse. The patent slip was a clever new invention which allowed the yard's workers to fit a cradle below a vessel while afloat and then to haul it out of the water so that repairs could be undertaken on dry land. Journalists marvelled briefly in the 1820s at the unexpected sight of large ships travelling slowly up from the water onto land.

A year at sea, subjected to the stresses and strains of the ocean, the weather, manhandling and a range of hungry pests with a taste for timber, made routine repair work essential. If the *Paragon* was to remain seaworthy and safe, her copper sheathing would need to be replaced at intervals throughout her working life, along with more frequent visits to have her planking repaired, masts checked and her standing rigging and sails maintained.

For a small business like Kelsick Wood & Sons, such repair work could be a lifeline, and it was another activity protected by the much-derided Navigation Act, the broad and shifting set of restrictive policies which provided the country's mariners and shipyards with a degree of protection against foreign competition.

The pictures above are from the *Encyclopaedia Londeninsis* (1828) top row, left to right: brig, dogger, schooner; bottom row, left to right: ship, sloop, snow. The majority of vessels produced by Kelsick's yard were two-masted brigs, along with less frequent ships and single-masted sloops. There is no barque, unfortunately, which the author describes as a ship converted 'by stripping the mizen-mast of its yards and the sails belonging to them'. A ship by definition had three masts or more, all square-rigged. In practice, the term 'ship' was often applied to any large seagoing vessel, especially when used in conjunction with other terms, such as shipbuilding, ship owner, ship's bell ... Like the very best Georgian newspaper editor, this account will endeavour to adhere to the correct usage but begs a forgiving attitude towards occasional lapses.

Only a British yard could undertake maintenance on a British vessel. Repair by a foreign yard would invalidate its status as British and, in doing so, shut the door to a substantial range of colonial markets and commercial activity.[3]

A WALK THROUGH THE TOWN

The River Ellen rose high among the Lakeland peaks and drew a broad arc as it flowed west towards the Irish Sea. It approached Maryport through the gardens of Netherhall, the Senhouse family's sprawling home, and then meandered around the southern tip of the town, where it was greeted by a blast furnace, a glass factory and a paper mill, each of which arrived and then departed from the Ellen's banks during the eighteenth and nineteenth centuries. Shipyards filled much of this waterfront during Kelsick's time. Finally, with King Street to its right and Irish Street to its left, the river widened into Maryport harbour.

The town's coal infrastructure lay on the southern bank opposite Kelsick's shipyard, on the large flat area known as Glasson. Horse-drawn coal carts arrived on the wooden wagonways which led from the collieries inland, the tracks fanning

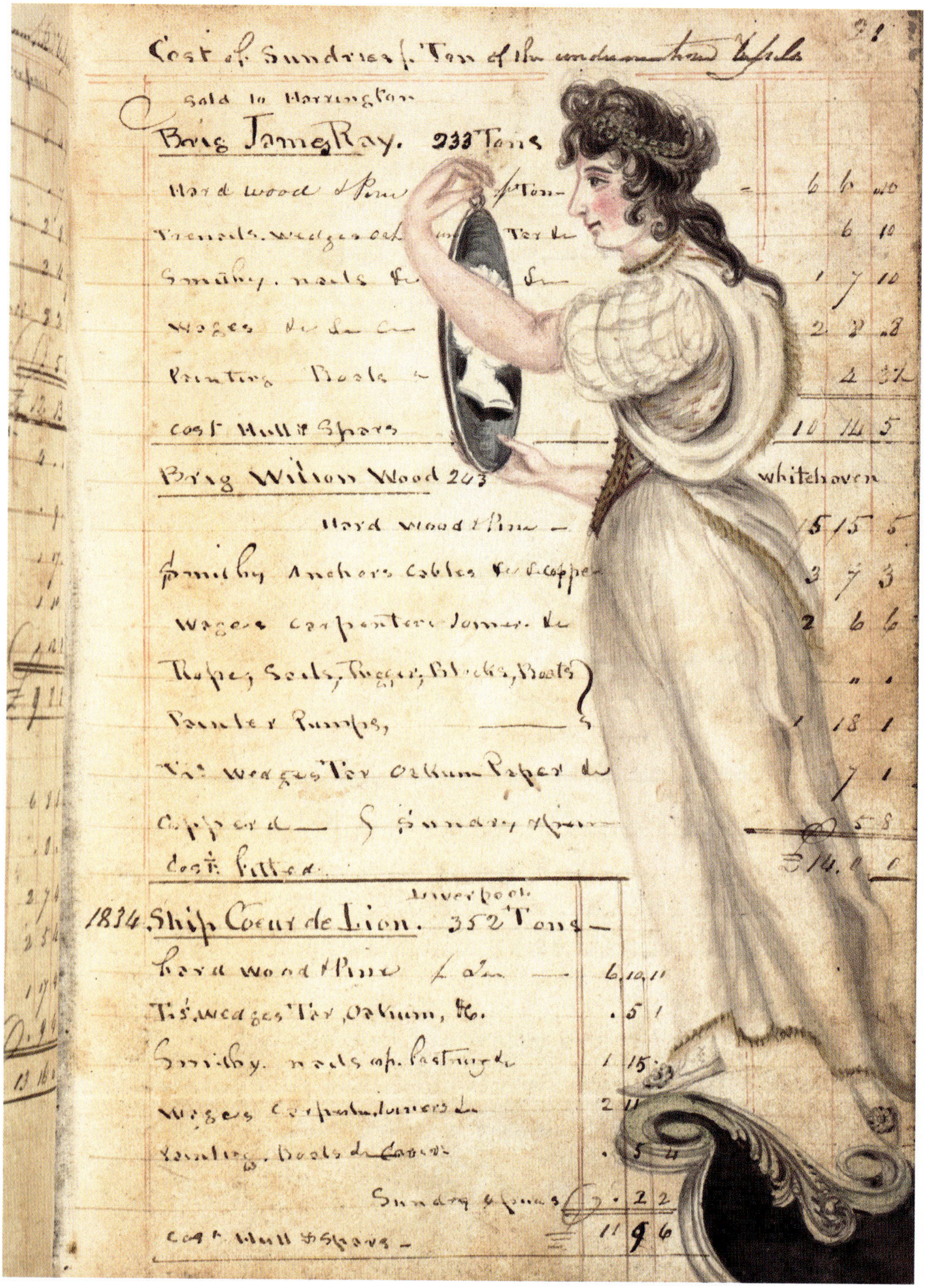

Kelsick reviews three projects, the *James Ray*, the *Wilton Wood* and the *Coeur de Lion*. He notes down the actual cost per ton for each vessel, considering everything from hard woods and pine, trunnels and wedges, tar and oakum, as well as iron work and the yard's wages. For the *James Ray*, the cost per ton was £10 14*s*. 5*d*. Unsurprisingly, timber was the greatest expense, followed by wages and the smithy.

out to points along the harbour wall, where coal brigs and sloops waited to be loaded.

The coal vessels and shipbuilders did not have the harbour entirely to themselves. Maryport had a sizeable fishing fleet, catching herring and cod in the seas beyond. Stocks of herring in the Solway Firth could ebb and flow but were still abundant in a good year.

The town's principal street was Senhouse Street, which climbed up the incline behind the harbour. From there, a tight grid pattern of side streets spreads across the slopes of Camp Hill to the north and Castle Hill to the south.

New towns built by industrialists were common in the north of England at this time, typified in many minds by the swathes of identical terraced houses which surrounded Lancashire's textile mills. Maryport's story was rather different. Humphrey Senhouse was a man with an eye on the fees and rents his enterprise might generate, rather than an industrialist or an urban developer. Although he is credited by many with building the town itself, his men built relatively little. Senhouse laid out the grid pattern of the streets and then leased parcels of land to Maryport's new residents, who bought one or more narrow, rectangular plots and then set about building upon them.

Budget constraints invariably capped any grander ambitions, but no two developments were quite the same. Some were faced with painted plaster, while others retained their sandstone façade, iron oxide giving the stone its ochre hue. The stucco door and window surrounds were of a colour of the owner's choosing. Some owners inscribed initials and dates above the doors of their new homes, helping today's historians plot out the town's early expansion. An occasional larger residence stood among the small, terraced houses, still conforming to the layout of the gridded streets but distinct in its scale, height and ornamentation.

Accentuated by the hilly terrain and uninterrupted by greenery, the ordered streets of Kelsick's new home presented a patchwork of different colours and details. It was a provincial but distinctly urban environment, designed for function. There was no space for trees, front gardens or grass other than that around the churchyard. The intentional laying out of parks and green spaces would be an endeavour more common in the Victorian years.

The Down Street area behind Kelsick's shipyard had a character of its own, but not necessarily for desirable reasons. The travel writer Richard Ayton was distinctly unimpressed when he visited in 1814, five years before Kelsick's arrival. Ayton takes the tone of an exasperated parent looking at a bedroom they had tidied only the day before. Maryport was a new town, barely sixty years old. How had it got into this state already?

> The upper town is well built and regularly laid out, the houses neat and the streets airy and spacious, but the lower division is as wretched as may be, betraying a condition of more shabbiness and filthiness than one should have supposed it could have fallen into in half a century.

WILLIAM RUSSELL AND LIFE IN MARYPORT

Visitors from more affluent Cumbrian centres such as Carlisle or Penrith may have entered the town with a certain trepidation. Maryport was a town with an edge to it. Landowners like Senhouse, businessmen like Wood and Huddleston, and the town's merchants and shopkeepers might find profit in it, but much of the population lived closer to the breadline. Work for the town's miners, shipwrights, tanners and seamen was often tough, physically demanding and badly paid.

There was also the frequent churn of temporary visitors, arriving from the collieries inland or from the sea aboard merchant vessels and fishing boats. Anecdotally, every second house had a parrot or a monkey, so great was the number of seafaring families.

Each new arrival in the harbour brought a fresh crew of men looking for a tavern to mark their return to land. Options in the town were many and varied. White's Directory from 1829 lists twenty-seven inns and taverns under Maryport, including the Sailor's Return, the Rigger's Arms and three called the Ship. Beyond these were numerous small, informal tap rooms, serving home-brewed beer direct from the barrel. The Golden Lion Inn on Senhouse Street provided a more refined meeting place. By turns a hotel, a restaurant and an inn, it was a favoured location for ship auctions, launch day parties and municipal gatherings.

In May 1896, William Russell, a retired ropemaker born and raised in the town, took to the stage at the old courthouse with a handful of notes and regaled the audience with recollections of his youth. His focus was broad but centred, conveniently for our purposes, on Maryport in 1832, the midpoint of Kelsick's tenure at the yard.

William was a boy of eight when the men at Kelsick Wood & Sons worked on the *Paragon*. He was the son of a local master mariner, Joseph, who for twenty years sailed the routes from Maryport to Dublin and Belfast as captain of the schooner *Mary and Frances*, another product of the Wood family's business. As men of standing in the tight-knit community, Kelsick and William's father Joseph would have been acquainted. Whether viewed as a blessing or a curse, one constant of life in a small town is that everyone knows each other's business.

William's handwritten account of Maryport in 1832 is now in the Carlisle Archive. It reads partly as local history and partly as a melancholy call to arms to recapture the town's former glory. His words are rough and crowd-pleasingly bawdy in places, but they reveal a lot about the community in which Kelsick, Mary and their children lived.

As William speaks, it becomes clear that, for all Humphrey Senhouse's aspirations of a modern town laid out on a clean grid pattern, facilities in the 1830s remained distinctly rudimentary, even seven decades after Senhouse's project had begun.

Behind the eclectic charm of the town's neat streets, the reality of life within the small, terraced houses was rather darker. When John Spear reported on the state of Maryport's sanitation to the Local Government Board in 1882, he described a town largely unchanged since Kelsick's day. Houses were typically cramped and claustrophobic, often severely over-crowded. Ventilation was poor, with windows routinely sealed shut, and many houses were filthy, with a strong smell of human waste in the damp air. Spear wrote that the town still had no effective sewer system. Many residents resorted to pail-closets, often no more than a wooden seat above a bucket. A cart travelled the streets most days to collect waste, with residents bringing their pails of excrement to the front door. Others emptied their waste directly into the town's open gutters. The memory of the stench seems to hang in Spear's words, and he writes, 'In many of the dwellings the rooms are extremely small; the filthiness of them is really shocking; and the foetor of them often such as to compel an immediate retreat from the opened door.'[4]

Behind each square of terraced housing lay a yard, accessed through an arched passage. The Wood family boat yard between Strand Street and King Street was just such a space, where the sailmaker, riggers and smithy occupied an area hidden by houses. Many yards were home to a variety of unsanitary enterprises, tallow factories, pig sties and stables among them. Around the edge of some yards was an inner ring of houses, built back-to-back with those facing the street. The dense arrangement of crowded houses, filthy yards, pungent tanneries and open sewers all added to the town's distinctive aroma.

The drinking water for most residents still came from shared pumps and, inevitably, the threat of disease loomed large among the poverty and squalor. Ships converged on the town from all corners of the world and, at a time of limited medical understanding and no antibiotics, the risk of the plague, cholera and other contagious diseases was ever present. Maryport was hit hard when the first outbreaks of cholera reached England in 1832, while workmen at Kelsick Wood & Sons were constructing the *James Ray*. William recalls the outbreak more than once. He even remembers the name of the first death in the town, 'a woman named Dobie in the lower part of Kirkby Street'.

Kelsick and others in the yard may not have appreciated the heightened risk that they faced. Much of the town's waste found its way into the Ellen, upstream of North Harbour. While most would be carried out to sea, a weak summer current could see slower-moving items brought back in with the returning tide.

The town offered a lot for the young William's keen eyes to take in. He describes travelling shows performing on the green, mountebanks or charlatans selling their potions, and games of marbles or pitch and toss. There is warmth in the picture William Russell paints, and a more rounded community emerges from amid his tales of hardship. Residents were resilient and hardworking, as they had to be, many of them fighting to keep their families out of poverty.

From his modern-day vantage point of 1896, William is quite insistent that the town's sanitation has improved so greatly in the intervening years that there is no longer any excuse for poor personal hygiene: 'Today the town is sewered. We have

Several portraits scattered among Kelsick's journals reflect a shifting ethnic diversity in Maryport, such as the seaman with straw hat, open collar and gold earring, painted with the stern of a ship beneath him.

a plentiful supply of good water, leaving no excuse for having either dirty houses or dirty clothes, nor even dirty persons.'

Spring was the busiest time of year, when ships were fitting out for the North American trade. Local pride ran deep, with a strong sense of duty to buy from local tradesmen and businesses, to keep what little wealth there was within the community, 'Everyone was anxious to spend their money in the town, and let their own townspeople have the full benefit of it. Would that it was more so today. ... where you make the money, there you ought to spend it.'

Among William's many anecdotes, one in particular bears repeating. He recalls how vessels arriving with cattle from Ireland had a no-fuss technique for accelerating the unloading process. Rather than entering the harbour to dock, seamen wrestled each cow to the deck and rolled it over the side of the ship and into the sea. The startled animal would swim towards the nearest land, where the town's bullock men stood waiting.

ETHNIC DIVERSITY

A small town in 1830s Cumberland might seem an unlikely place to look for ethnic diversity, but Britain's port communities could be surprisingly multicultural, even in the mid-nineteenth century.

As an ocean wanderer like the *Eliza Heywood* or the *Stirlingshire* travelled between the world's ports, the ship's company would rarely remain unchanged. The hazards were numerous during a long voyage. At sea a man might slip from the mast, be swept overboard or fall ill. In port, he might be dismissed, arrested or desert. Each departure meant a vacant post for the master to fill. This steady turnover of seamen meant that a crew returning to a British port might be quite different to that which had departed many months previous.

In his book *Black Salt: Seafarers of African descent on British ships*, Ray Costello describes the racial diversity to be found in Liverpool's extensive Sailortown community, close to the Albert Dock. He comments that some inhabitants would have been short-term visitors, seamen in port for only as long as their ship, but for others it was home.

Among Maryport's residents at this time was John Kent (1805–86), considered to have been Britain's first black police officer. The early life of John's father Thomas is uncertain, but he is thought to have arrived in Whitehaven from the West Indies and worked for the Senhouse family at Calder Abbey, 'as a slave'. After several years, he married Eleanor Kent and moved to Carlisle. Three of their sons lived and worked in Maryport during the 1830s, although who was there first is unclear. Thomas found work as a gardener, Joseph as a stonemason and John, the youngest of the three, took a post as a police constable in 1835.

John's career is explored by Ray Greenhow in his biography *Britain's First Black Policeman*, describing his investigations and arrests, and his interventions in thefts, riots and assaults. John Kent left Maryport in April 1837 and moved to Carlisle, where he lived with his wife Mary and continued his career in law enforcement.

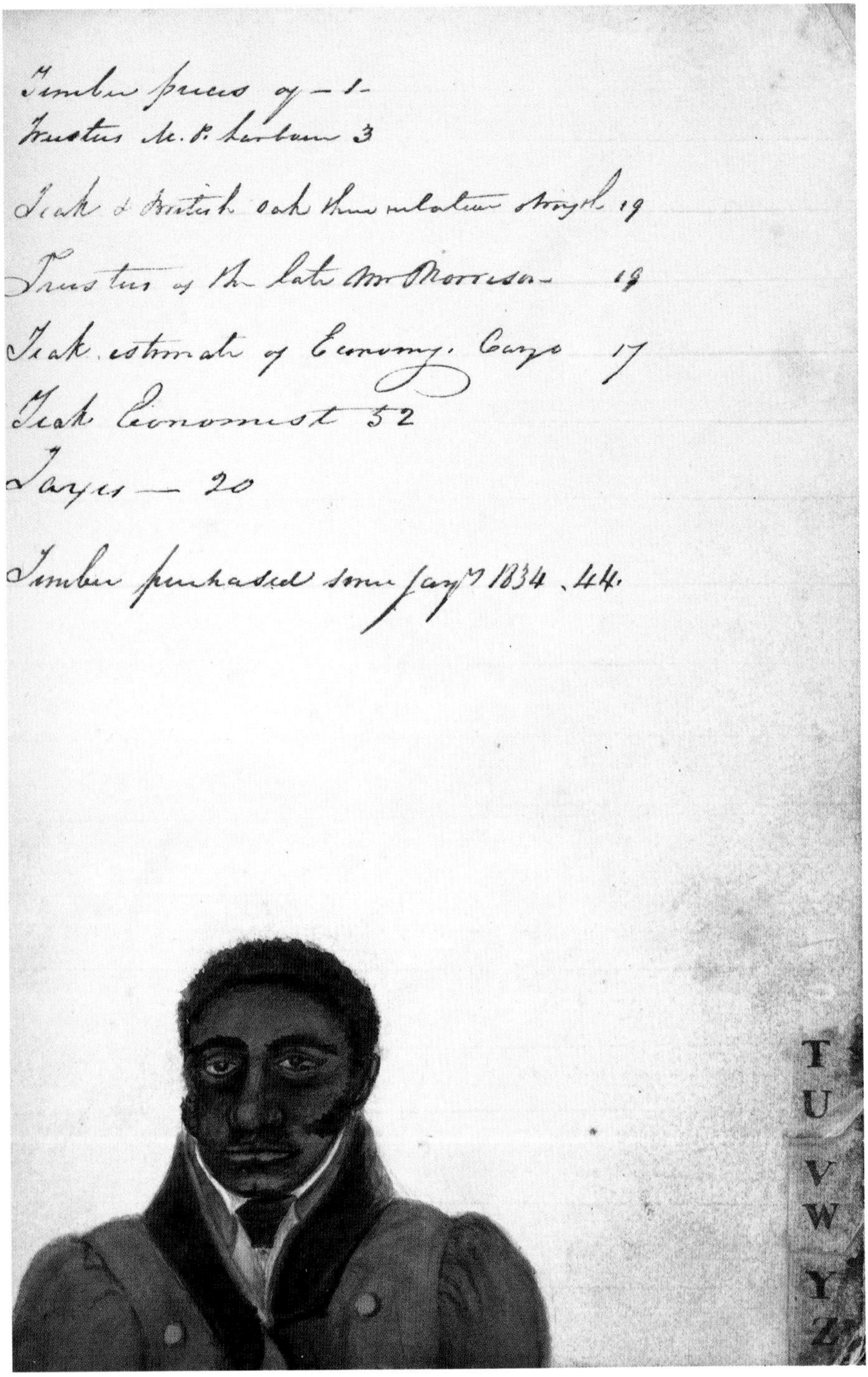

The handsome man in the red coat and blue waistcoat is perhaps too smartly dressed for a police constable's budget, but John Kent would have been a familiar figure in Kelsick's part of town. The local police lock-up was a cave carved into the hillside behind the Wood family shipyard, 'a sad damp place to put any human being into', as William Russell remembered it.

THE ARRIVAL OF THE LLOYD'S REGISTER SURVEYOR

The *Paragon* was one of the last of the yard's vessels to be built away from the critical eye of a surveyor from Lloyd's Register. By the time the Dawson family returned to the yard in 1836 with a second project, the *Campbell*, the rules were quite different.

The system of ship registration had originated in Lloyd's Coffee House in Lombard Street, London, in 1760, its purpose being to provide merchants and underwriters with a source of reliable information about the vessels they might want to charter or insure. Each new vessel's hull was rated by letter and its equipment by number, and 'A1 at Lloyd's' appeared prominently on many listings.

As initially conceived, a vessel's A1 rating was lost after a fixed number of years, regardless of the original build quality or the state of subsequent maintenance. There was also a rather outrageous geographical bias. While ships built in London retained their A1 status for twelve or thirteen years, a yard in the north of England would see its vessels rated A1 for seven or eight years only, putting them at an immediate competitive disadvantage.[5]

The system had unravelled when underwriters and shipowners locked horns on how it should operate. After a bitter dispute, Lloyd's Register was reconstituted in 1834, bringing with it new rules of classification.

The revised system was based around the materials used and the quality of construction. It was designed to encourage shipyards to build durable vessels, and owners to repair them. Annual surveys were to be undertaken to review the grade assigned to existing ships.

Henceforth, a Lloyd's Register-appointed surveyor would visit Kelsick's shipyard three times during the construction of each new vessel. The first survey would come after the frame was assembled, the second when the beams were put in but before decks were laid, and a final visit when work on the vessel was complete.

Alongside these intrusive new surveys, the new classification system also brought some good news. The weighting in favour of London was removed. Kelsick Wood & Sons could now compete on equal terms with every yard in the country.

Many years later, in 1858, the chairman of Lloyd's Register, Thomas Chapman, reflected on the problems with the old system, 'There was no inducement for the north of England to build good ships, while there was every inducement for the south of England to build bad ones.' Lloyd's Register, he said, had been set up with 'the purpose of correcting this evil'.

The local Lloyd's Register surveyor, Thomas Braithwaite, submitted his report on the *Campbell* shortly after her launch in 1837 and confirmed that he had surveyed her during construction. His two-page report seems impressively thorough to a modern layman's eyes. He goes into great detail on the timber used and the thickness of the planks at different points, and he measures the copper bolt fastenings. He lists the sail types and sizes, assesses the rigging and the cables, and itemises the anchors, of which there are five, all of proper weight. Two paragraphs of comments at the end go into more exhaustive detail before Braithwaite concludes, 'This vessel was built under the inspection of the owner and is in every way a well-finished vessel.'

Rules continued 45

Keel & Kelsons	Tons 150 – 300	Tons 500
Keelsided	9	13
moulded below the rabbet	7	10
Main Kelson sided	10	14
moulded — — —	10	14
Scarphs one [illegible] Kelson	5	7
	4½	6

with Riders [illegible] Timber in
shifts [illegible] of 200 Tons and
Ships of [illegible] to be 1/7 of the
upwards [illegible] breadth and
[illegible] under 200 Tons
in Ships [illegible] 1/6 main breadth
to be

Outside Plank
above the light water mark to be English, African Oak, East Indian Teak, or Red Cedar.

Plank below Light water Mark
white Oak. Elm or Beech not be wrought higher than the first futtock heads. —
the clamps, spirkettings, shelf pieces, and ceiling to be English or African Oak, or Teak.

See the otherside —

Kelsick carefully transcribed Lloyd's Register's revised rules into his journals. He found space for his pictures alongside them, but he resisted the temptation to add further notes, doodles or calculations.

All looks good, except for a worrying pencil comment at the foot of his report, added by a reviewer with the initials GB, 'I cannot comprehend the description given of the fastening of this vessel. I suspect that the surveyor himself does not understand what he writes about.'[6]

On the basis of the surveyor's muddled report, Lloyd's Register classified the *Campbell* as A1 for eleven years only, rather than the full twelve. Faced with a 'much disappointed' Kelsick, Braithwaite wrote once more to London and sought to remedy his mistake. Fortunately for both shipbuilder and surveyor, the General Committee reviewed Braithwaite's fresh comments and upgraded its classification.

FIGUREHEADS

The Admiralty had sought to limit the use of carved figureheads on naval ships since the late eighteenth century, but their popularity remained undimmed among the owners of Britain's merchant vessels. Some depicted animals or mythical creatures, but people were the most common subject, among them monarchs, classical heroes and contemporary figures, often relating to the name of the ship itself. Some vessels carried a billethead instead, decorative woodwork attached directly to the bow of the ship, often formed of curlicues or rosettes. Others carried neither.[7]

The yard routinely commissioned pieces from local carvers such as James Brooker and John Askew, while on certain projects Kelsick himself took the lead. The *Cumberland Pacquet* was characteristically unrestrained in its praise of his creations for the *Eliza Heywood* in 1833:

> The carving of the head and stern has been executed by Mr Wood, sen., and is universally admired for the design as well as for the tasty execution. She has a very beautiful billet head, on each side of which is a naiad blowing a shell, and underneath is the quaint but appropriate motto 'Noli mi tangere' – touch me not.

One perennial favourite was the partially clothed woman. The presence of an actual woman on board might have been bad luck in some eyes, but superstition also held that a semi-naked female on the bow could protect a ship in a storm.

This was the last real golden era for the wooden figurehead. A revival followed later in the century with the rise of the streamlined tea clipper, but the days of the figurehead carver were numbered. The steady shift to steam power and the straight, unfussy lines of iron-hulled ships spelled the end of the protruding bowsprit, below which the colourful figurehead had traditionally been attached.

MOTTOS

Not all forms of ship heraldry were rendered obsolete so quickly. Even today, a British naval ship is entitled to its own badge or emblem, often with a motto incorporated. Kelsick transcribed his list of favoured mottos from one journal to the next.

Some, like 'God defends me from danger' or 'May Providence be our guide', are more akin to prayers, while others are more patriotic. Mottos like *Commercia noris que presidia nostratum libertatem* ('Commerce and shipping, the safeguards of our

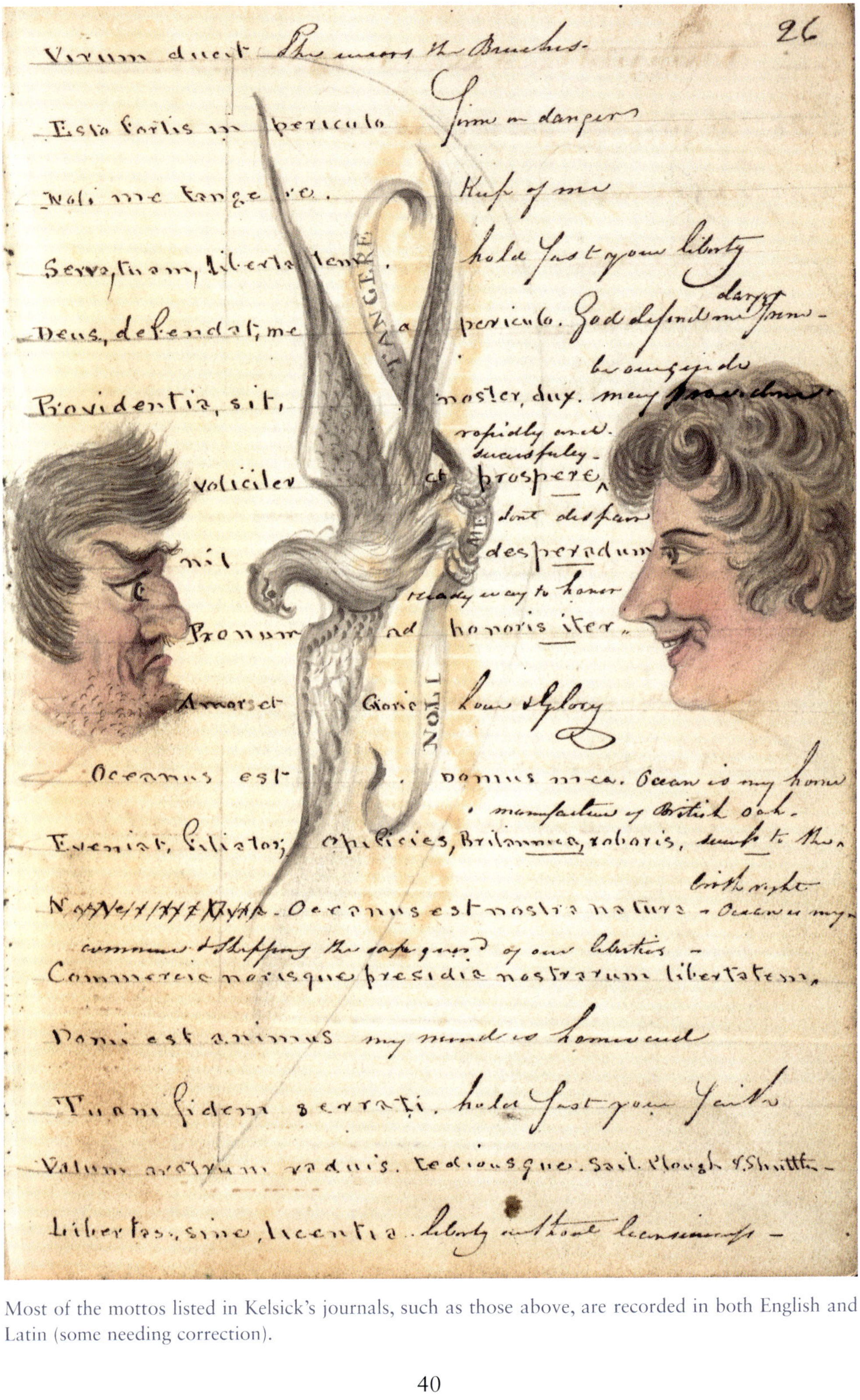

Most of the mottos listed in Kelsick's journals, such as those above, are recorded in both English and Latin (some needing correction).

liberties') and *Oceanus est nostra natura* ('The ocean is our birth right') are reminders of the important role of the merchant service in securing Britain's hard-won dominance of the waves. In the same vein, *Velum aratrum radius tediousque* ('Sail, Plough and Shuttle') gives a nod to the spinning jenny which had revolutionised textile production.

Eveniat filiator opificies Britannica arboris ('Success to the manufacturers of British oak') played on the nation's pride in its mighty oak trees. The symbolic importance of the tree had been heightened during the long war with France when the Royal Navy's fleet of oak giants had formed the country's 'wooden walls'.

Kelsick even offered his clients a bit of bumper sticker humour with *Virum ducit* ('She wears the breeches').

Together, the carved ornamentation, the decorative flourishes and the heraldic badges and mottos combined to give each ship a character of its own. The figurehead might also help an illiterate sailor find his way back to the right vessel.

IN THE BOAT YARD

In the boat yard on the opposite side of Strand Street, the sailmaker made his careful calculations based on the size and rigging of the vessel under construction. A two-masted brig might carry roughly 400 square yards of sail. The pattern for each sail was chalked onto the loft floor before the heavy sections of canvas were cut, stitched, hemmed and finished. Bell & Co. supplied sailcloth from Whitehaven, 14 miles down the Cumberland coast.[8]

In the rigging loft, riggers prepared the many yards of standing and running rigging that the new vessel would require. For the *Paragon*, the order for much of this cordage went to Brocklebank & Co. in Whitehaven, but at other times the business was given to the family firm of Wilton Wood & Co. in Liverpool.

Standing rigging, often tarred black for protection, supported the masts and bowsprit, and had to be properly tensioned to ensure the structural integrity of the vessel. Running rigging included all the various ropes used during navigation to raise, lower and control the sails. Fully rigged, a brig could require a remarkable 6 miles of cordage of all types and diameter.

The yard's supply chain had to be diverse and international to satisfy this continual hunger for materials, but not all items were purchased at a great distance. Some suppliers were distinctly local. Within the town of Maryport itself, Thomas Tickle supplied chains and copper nails from his local foundry. Brass fittings came from Lewis Wilmot in Whitehaven, also home to the carver John Askew, who received the commission for work on the *Wilton Wood*. Further to the south, there were merchants in Liverpool competing to provide whatever a Cumberland shipbuilder required, like Thomas Rodick, who delivered the copper sheeting used to clad hulls below the waterline.

It was down to the yard's foreman, James Fell, to bring the labours of all these men together, as not all were required at the same time. As the cold, wet winter gave way to spring, the shipwrights' work on the *Paragon* was nearing completion. Much of what remained could be undertaken once she was on the water. Once the *Paragon*'s hull had been painted, the yard could prepare for launch day.

Everyone in the boat yard worked to the sounds of the blacksmith's rhythmic hammering. The smithy was an expensive part of the yard to operate and demanded large quantities of coking coal, which burned especially hot. Kelsick calculated that in 1835 alone, his smithy had consumed an impressive sixty wagons of coal, costing a hefty £55 10*s*. for the year. On the same page, a worried-looking dog runs away with its tail between its legs, hoping to avoid a beating.

MARYPORT'S MASTER SHIPBUILDERS

Kelsick's late uncle, William Wood, had been the first to build ships at Maryport but others had soon followed. Next had come John Peat, who had run his yard on the banks of the River Ellen since at least 1785, followed by the Middletons, Isaac and Joseph. The most recent arrival had been a partnership between Joseph Huddleston and John Ritson, former manager of Peat's yard. The Wood and Ritson-Huddleston yards were the larger of the four.

The relationship between the town's shipbuilders was likely a mix of rivalry and support. The four businesses were competing for clients, certainly, but they were small fish in a much larger pond. There were yards like theirs along the Cumbrian coast and beyond, many of them also courting the same clients in Whitehaven and Liverpool.

The yards were also competing for labour. Each required a substantial workforce of shipwrights and other craftsmen, and a large number of apprentices and manual workers for all the lifting, heaving and general grunt work common to a pre-mechanised industry. The harbour and the shipyards were at the heart of the small town's economy, and the master shipbuilders held the fortunes of many of the town's families in their hands. The Wood yard alone provided employment for 200 workers. It may have been a challenge in the early years to staff the only yard in the town but by 1830, four shipyards and an array of ancillary businesses ensured a larger pool of resources.

When Kelsick makes a brief foray into diarist in 1834, there are encouraging signs of collaboration between the town's rivals. Maryport's shipyards may have been in competition with each other, but a thriving local shipbuilding industry helped everyone:

> Tuesday, January 14th. A remarkably wet morning, wind south, carved the other dolphin. Dined with son John and met Mr Huddleston. Messrs Ritson agreed to lend us 2000ft teak till ours arrived. Fair the latter part of the day. The sloop *Lark* on shore to the south of the harbour, likely to be stranded.

The close relationship between the town's shipbuilders sometimes hit a more sombre note. It is tempting to portray Kelsick Wood & Sons as a contented workplace where workers and management rubbed along seamlessly, all overseen by the benevolent Mr Wood, notebook in hand, the scent of sawdust in the air and the sounds of the yard floating in through the office window. It may have been that way at times, but it was not always so.

Several decades had passed since the French Revolution, but the fear it had struck among British law makers had lingered on the statute books. Concerned that similar revolutionary sentiment could spread to British workers, Parliament had passed the Combination Acts of 1799 and 1800, outlawing trade unions and largely removing the opportunity for workers to express their demands in any coordinated way.

The Acts were widely despised and were finally repealed in 1824 after extensive lobbying. The consequence, as workers began to exercise their new-found freedom, was perhaps inevitable. Within a year, a wave of industrial disputes brought the country to its knees. Strikers called for long-overdue improvements in pay, hours and working conditions, or walked out in solidarity with workers in other cities or in other industries. Dire warnings about economic repercussions and foreign competition had little effect and, by July 1825, Britain was in a state of near shutdown.

Five years earlier, at St Peter's Field in Manchester, a large public protest had been dispersed by cavalry troops, who rode with sabres drawn into the crowd of thousands. Eighteen people were killed in what became known as the infamous 'Peterloo Massacre'. On that day in 1819, the protestors had been campaigning for electoral reform rather than working conditions, but beneath each protest lay a familiar sense of injustice.

Parliament hurried through a new Act, which again limited workers' rights to take industrial action, but the fuse of discontent had been lit. Legal or otherwise, disputes between workers and employers continued throughout the rest of the year and relations grew ever more fragile.

Matters came to a head at Kelsick Wood & Sons on the morning of 21 October. The facts are obscured by highly partisan reporting but, according to the *Carlisle Patriot*, shipwrights walked out in a dispute because the Wood family had been 'so unreasonable as to refuse their servants the power of dictating the internal management of the yard!', concluding with apparent dismay that, 'Matters are thus coming to a pretty pass'. Things were no better in Whitehaven, where the gates at the Brocklebank yard remained closed after the owner was knocked to the ground in a confrontation with his employees.[9]

Cumberland's master shipbuilders met at the Black Lion in Whitehaven in late October to discuss how to wrest back control. They announced their resolutions in the local newspapers. In consequence of the 'tyrannical and disorderly conduct' of the union members, they declared, the shipbuilders owed it to themselves, to the public and to society as a whole, to cease employment of union men and to increase the daily rate for a non-union shipwright to 4*s*. Unfortunately, the heavy-handed measures backfired and encouraged several more non-union workers to down tools in solidarity.

The dispute rumbled on through the dark winter months but with the arrival of spring 1826, the *Cumberland Pacquet* reported that union support was fading. The *Astrea* had been taken up the patent slip for repair at Kelsick Wood & Sons and workers were returning to the yard.

The strikes might be over, but that did not bring an end to the rhetoric, as rival newspaper editors continued to state their case. The *Cumberland Pacquet* warned that owners would show preference to men who had worked throughout the dispute, while the *Trades Free Press*, the one paper to have been vocal in its support for the unions, called on workers to remember their collective power:

> Men of Cumberland, look to your Union. It is a city of refuge for the worn out and disabled shipwright; whilst it will be a shield against the malignant shafts of your enemies. It is your only anchor of hope, and if you lose that, all is lost for ever.

Quite whether Kelsick shared their view that employment in his yard constituted a 'malignant shaft' can only be a matter of conjecture.

Cordage For No 40 continued

14

1835

March 26 Topmast shrouds 3½ Rope a full Tackle

Fore Sheets 26 fathoms 3½ Rope

Main Sheets 27 fathoms 3¼ do

double Main Tacks 24 fathoms 3¼ do

Fore tacks 34 feet each 4½ at the Neck

30 fathoms 4¼ Rope 2 Coils Lanyard Rope

2 Coils of 14 Yarn Rope. 2 do of 12 do do

3 do of 10 do do 4 do of 3 do do

4 do of 6 do do 4 doz 4 do do

4 do of 3 do do 2 Buoy Ropes 15 & 20 fath each

one doz Lanks Amberline 1 doz 3 thread

Spunyarn 5 doz. 2 thread Spunyarn

3 doz Balls housing 5 doz

Balls marling. 5 doz of fine

Block strap. Spunyarn

ends of Shrouds &c

For the 19 fathoms of

Jib Stay 4½ Rope

4 Strands

2 Hawsers

90 Fathoms each

The cordage for the *Paragon* gets a page to itself, with everything listed out in fathoms and yards. Kelsick allows his words to fade into the dark shading in front of the young lady's face. His final volume, held by the National Maritime Museum, shows that the illustrations came first. The pictures run on to the end, while the shipyard entries finish several pages earlier.

LAUNCH DAY

Those who did not work at Kelsick's shipyard, or have cause to visit, might still observe its activities with interest as they went about their business. Jonathan Douglas might note the frame of a vessel rising beyond the rooftops of King Street as he walked on Camp Hill. The young William Russell could peer through gaps in the yard's fence, and returning fishermen might watch the shipwrights at work when entering the harbour with a hold full of Atlantic cod. For all these casual glimpses, however, nothing presented an opportunity like a launch day.

Launch days have always been special occasions in shipbuilding towns. They represent the day when the labours of so many in the town are placed at the fore and celebrated.

The launch of the *Collingwood* in January 1829 was recorded in a contemporary painting, later copied by William Mitchell. While onlookers assemble on North Pier, final preparations are being made in the yard to the left, beneath the green of Camp Hill. The Union Flag flies at the bow and the Red Ensign at the stern, staging has been removed and guests are visible on the main deck. The winter weather may have dampened the scale of the festivities, but a crowd gathers regardless, with growing excitement as the hour approaches.

The *Collingwood*'s launch had been in doubt just a few weeks earlier when a vicious gale hit the Cumberland coast. Powerful westerly winds had united with an unusually high tide, herding large waves towards the shore and pushing the angry sea ever higher. Kelsick and his men could only look on helplessly, entertaining 'great fears' that the vulnerable *Collingwood* would be swept off her berth. Fortunately, the new vessel had remained in position and a month later the launch could proceed.[10]

Contemporary newspapers give lengthy accounts of several of the yard's launch days, that of the *Eliza Heywood* in particular, and we can picture the launch of the *Paragon* in 1835 as being choreographed along similar lines:

Long before the crowds and dignitaries assemble on Saturday, 16 May, the yard's carpenters have transferred the weight of the brig from the keel blocks to a cradle beneath the hull. For all those associated with her construction, this will be a day of celebration mixed with anxiety. The motion of entering the water will put the first real stress on the new hull. There can be no dress rehearsal. The shipwrights are about to discover whether the vessel they have constructed over many months is watertight, her structure sound and whether she sits as expected in the water.

The new vessel's owners, George Dawson and his nephew John, are among the honoured guests. The appointed hour is announced with 'Rule Britannia', or a similarly rousing tune, after which the *Paragon* and her crew are blessed in a short service. The guest appointed to christen the ship, often a woman and perhaps John Dawson's wife Elizabeth on this occasion, declares the new vessel's name to the crowd and breaks a bottle of wine across her bow. Taking their cue, workmen knock away the remaining wedges. Guns fire, the crowd cheers and, after the briefest moment of anticipation, the hull begins its journey down the slipway.

The Launch of the Collingwood from Kelsick Wood Yard, Maryport, William Mitchell of Maryport, 1884. Mitchell's painting is a copy of an older picture by W. Brown of Maryport and Jenkinson of Liverpool, painted at the time of the *Collingwood*'s launch in 1829. Only the hull will be launched at this point – the upper masts, the rudder, rigging and many other items will be brought in later, once the brig is moored. The frame of a second, smaller vessel is under construction to the left. The painting shows the limited space available for the yard behind North Harbour. The walled area to the right was leased to Kelsick Wood & Sons, certainly in the 1850s.

North Pier provided townsfolk and tourists with the perfect viewing gallery. It would have made for an impressive sight: the huge wooden structure slowly gathering speed, and the force of her bulk pushing the stern into the water, before rising up and driving a large wave outward.

With the *Paragon* now at rest, she can be moored alongside the quay. There is still much to be done before she is ready for her maiden voyage. Vessels were typically launched when they were still little more than attractively painted hulls, often to make way for the next project. Ballast must be added and the rudder hung. The heavy masts will be moved into position, and the standing and running rigging will also follow. Beyond that, the interior needs to be fitted out and cabins installed.

All that can wait until another day, though. For now, with the launch concluded, Kelsick, his family, the party of owners and local dignitaries can get down to the serious business of lunch. They adjourn to a nearby inn, where they take their time over their food, give speeches and make toasts. The *Paragon*'s launch has represented the day towards which so many have striven, and it is a well-deserved moment to enjoy.

A SHORT-LIVED DIARY

As 1834 arrived, Kelsick resolved to keep a diary, although his enthusiasm appears to have been limited. Many entries are brief and rather awkward. Retaining log-keeping habits from his younger years at sea, each day gets a brief report on the weather and wind direction but often little else. Across the nineteen pages, though, some of the more expansive entries give a glimpse of family life and activity in the yard. We learn a lot about Kelsick, although not as much perhaps as we might hope.

The yard is putting the finishing touches to the *Coeur de Lion* (vessel No. 37, as Kelsick generally calls it) at the time. Work has continued through the dark, wet winter and by January 1834, the build is drawing to a close. Just as Kelsick had carved pieces for the *Mary* and the *Eliza Heywood*, so he does once more, this time carving two dolphins for the new ship's stern. Further ornamentation is delivered from Liverpool. There is growing interest in the town as the new ship nears completion, and Humphrey Senhouse calls by to show a guest what the men of the yard are constructing.

The weather is causing problems for the workmen as attention shifts to more delicate and precise tasks. Much of January is cold but fine, although painting the hull while the skies are threatening rain leads to problems.

- Friday, January 3rd. *Union* steamer arrived. A dark rainy morning, wind South West. Brought the undermentioned articles for Captain Fisher's new ship, copper, nails, sheathing... &c. A meeting of the owners of the *Arrow*, Liverpool trader, held this day at 2pm. Agreed to have her sold. John out at a game party. Weather was stormy through the day. Received a letter from Nelson.
- Monday 6th. Fair morning, wind SW. Nearly calm ... Son John & Self dined with Mr Inman this day. No letters or papers this day. H. Senhouse Junior with a foreign Sir called to see the new ship of Captain Fisher. A beautiful winter's day throughout. 10pm, rain and wind at SSW. *Saint George* arrived at 9pm.
- Monday 13th. Wet morning. Fair from 12 noon, wind SW, carved a dolphin for the badges of new ship, no. 37. Capt Heywood came over, fine evening.
- Thursday 16th. Clear morning, wind S. West but showery. No letters, 2 papers for Miss Watts. Began painting the new ship. A wet night and dreadful gale of wind. Paint sadly spoiled.
- Friday 17th. Fair morning wind at S.W., very showery like. Steamer arrived with carved stern and rigging for No. 37. Wife arrived from Flimby Lodge by the coach.

Kelsick's diary shows the fragility of the yard's supply chain. He is waiting on two cargo vessels and there are problems with both. The first is the *Saint George*, which arrives at Maryport on 6 January, with nails and copper, but without the spars which Kelsick has been expecting. The second is the *Johns*, returning from Sierra Leone. Kelsick follows reports of her progress closely but learns with disappointment in February that she has put into St Ubes, Portugal, leaky.

The personal and the professional can be hard to distinguish at times, particularly when it comes to dinner, when the business of the yard and the town are rarely

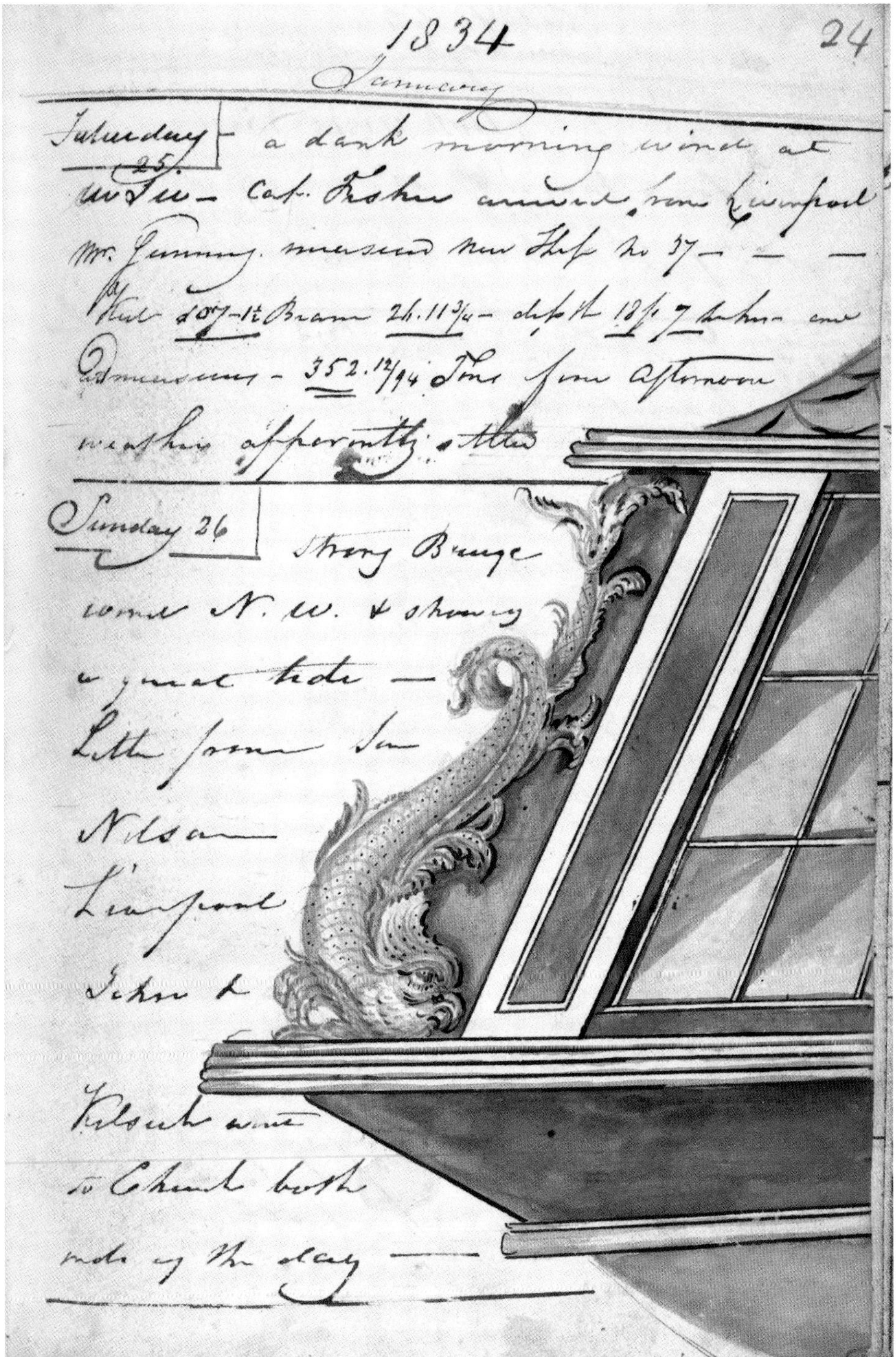

1834 24

January

Saturday 25 — a dark morning wind at
W.S.W. — Capt. Fisher arrived from Liverpool
Mr. [illegible] measured new Ship No 37 — — —
Keel 107-1/2 Beam 26.11 3/4 — depth 18 ft 7 inches [illegible]
Admeasures — 352.17/94 Tons fine afternoon
weather apparently settled

Sunday 26 strong Breeze
wind N.W. & showery
a great tide —
Letter from Sir
Nelson
Liverpool
John &
[illegible] went
to Church both
ends of the day —

While the bow of a vessel might display an eye-catching figurehead or billethead, with colourful trailboards flowing behind, the stern could be just as ornate. Dolphins were often stylised to resemble sea serpents, such as the one seen here.

far away. In the days preceding the *Coeur de Lion*'s launch, Kelsick dines with Captain Sumpton, her future master, and then William Fisher, her principal owner, who returns in the days which follow. Other dinner companions are mentioned, one day Mr Tolson, another day Mr Rodgers from Glasgow. Joseph Huddleston, now linked to Kelsick's family through marriage, also makes a regular appearance.

Much like the royal houses of Europe, personal unions bound together the town's rival shipbuilding dynasties: Kelsick's son John married Joseph's daughter Sarah Huddleston in 1831. Not to be confused with his half-brother, John Nelson, John became increasingly involved in the Maryport business from the 1820s onwards, although in Kelsick's diary, he is either playing cards or at game parties.

- Monday, January 20th. Dark morning but fair wind S.W. Capt Sumpton arrived from Liverpool, busy painting new ship. Read an account of the *Johns* having left Sierra Leone on the 20 Nov, therefore she is not yet due. Heavy rain all the afternoon, thick and dark. Capt Sumpton dined with us.
- Saturday 25th. A dark morning, wind at WSW. Captain Fisher arrived from Liverpool. Mr Gunning measured new ship No. 37 ... Fine afternoon, weather apparently settled.
- Monday 27th. Poor morning. Wind at WNW at ½ past 12pm. Launched the new ship *Coeur de Lion* for Messrs Fisher and Son, Liverpool. She made a beautiful launch and was moored opposite the Custom House ... Dined at Bowls, a large party and spent a pleasant day.

Kelsick's wife Mary remains opaque in her husband's diary. She is mentioned only infrequently, always as 'My wife', never by name. She does not appear to join Kelsick at church or for any of the dinners he describes. Of course, it may be that she simply slips beneath the diary's horizon. As his companion and wife of thirty-eight years, Kelsick may feel that her presence is to be assumed, needing no mention.

We learn that Kelsick is not an avid churchgoer, missing more Sunday services in January than he attends. By contrast, John and Kelsick Junior sometimes go twice, at both ends of the day. The town's principal church was St Mary's, a small country chapel with whitewashed walls and a short square tower, close to the Senhouse family's Netherhall mansion. The chapel's interior was a maze of private pews and wooden upper galleries, all bought and sold through the years by Maryport's wealthier parishioners. Social hierarchies held firm, even within the house of God.

The old chapel was replaced during the Victorian era to meet the needs of a fast-growing congregation. Burials in the churchyard ceased and all human remains were re-interred in a new cemetery.

A number of the original headstones remain at St Mary's, relocated to the edge of the grassy yard, where they stand looking inwards towards the church. Many have fared poorly through the last 200 years, their dark red sandstone eroded and inscriptions indistinct, masked by ivy, while others have toppled forward, their message now a secret between stone and soil. Others stand as proud as the day they were erected.

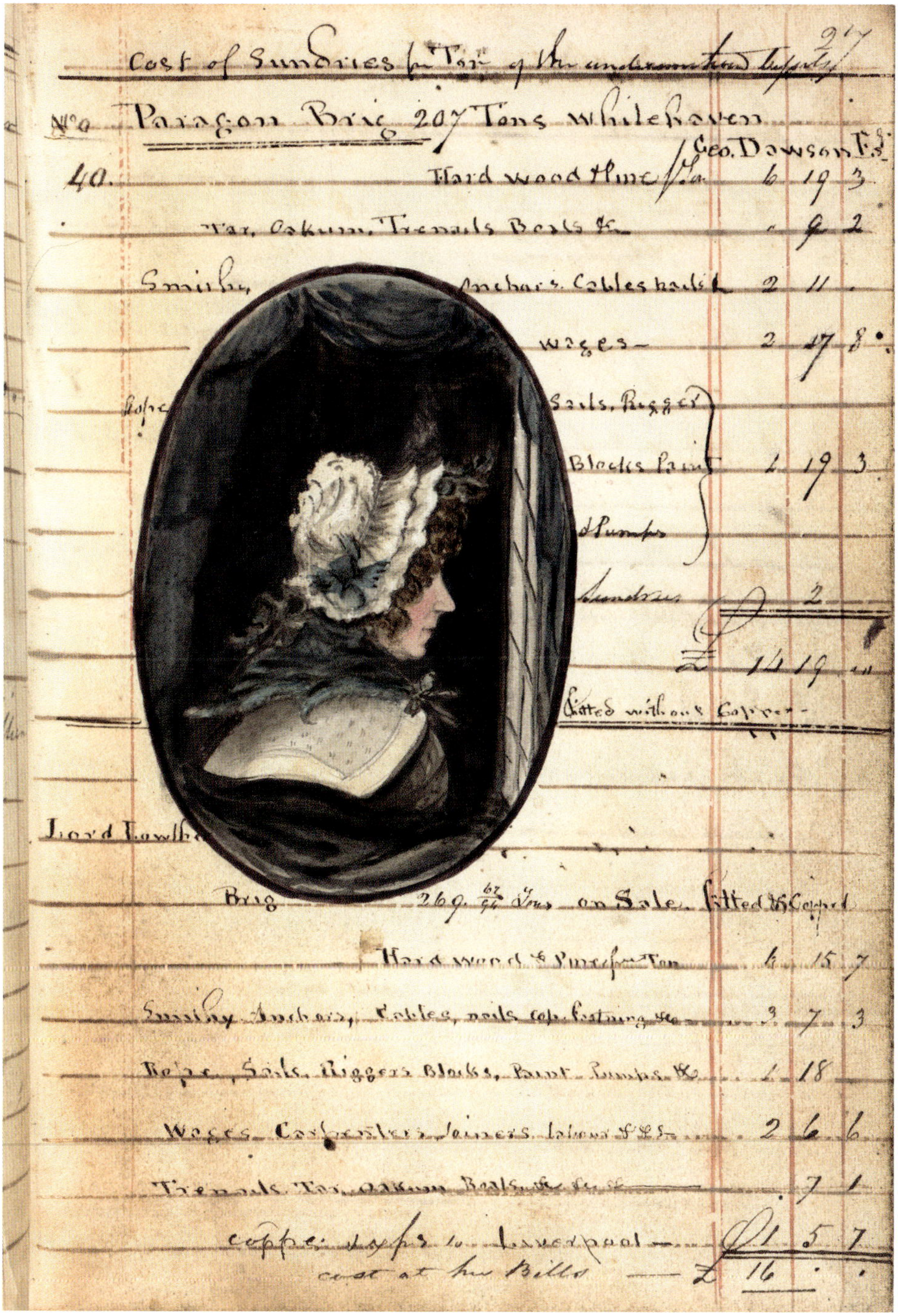

Two pictures of Kelsick's second wife Mary Inman share the same sense of isolation. In this portrait, Mary is alone in a dark room, looking out of a window. The colours are muted and Mary's clothes, bonnet and neck scarf appear like a barrier against the world. With the approximate dating of 1833, Kelsick was painting Mary not long after the untimely death of their son Wilton. A lonely husband, perhaps, searching for a connection with his distant, grieving wife.

Many of Maryport's best-known maritime families are represented. A search for the Wood family also reveals headstones and memorials for the Ritsons, Huddlestons and the Ismays of White Star and Titanic shipping fame. Sea captains appear in large numbers, like Captain Edward Bell ('Died at Sea on his Passage to Buenos Ayres, April the 27th, 1817'), whose stone leans against an ivy-covered wall in the northern corner. Another headstone is a testament to Maryport's dry Cumbrian humour, marking the grave of an unknown seaman reputedly found washed up on the shore in the 1800s, with 10*s*. in his pocket, 'Here lieth the body of 10/= Smyth. An Irishman. Aged 25'.

After the *Coeur de Lion*'s launch into North Harbour, her lower masts and ballast are brought into position and work to get her ready for sea can be completed. The strong winds and rain return as she sails for Liverpool in early March, and there follow an anxious few days before Kelsick receives news of her safe arrival.

- Wednesday, January 28th. Fresh breezy wind from NE to North. The *Coeur de Lion* got the three lower masts in, with a quantity of ballast. Gave in our terms for a new vessel to build of 450 tons to Mr Horsfall. Kelsick dined at Netherhall. Continued rain from 11am till midnight. On this day eve the *Mary* arrived.
- Tuesday, February 11th. Fair morning, wind SW. Sailed the *Coeur de Lion* under single reef'd topsails. Mr Rodgers from Glasgow dined with us. John and Mrs went to Workington in the evening.
- Thursday 13th. Fine day, wind NW. A family party to dinner. No account of the *Coeur de Lion* getting through to Liverpool. Rain began at 5pm and lasted all night.
- Friday 14th. Dark close morning, wind little or none from the westward. Middle and latter part remarkably fine. Several vessels sailed. Heard of the safe arrival of the *Coeur de Lion* at Liverpool.

Even those entries with just a brief weather report remind us of something important. Work in the yard continued regardless of the conditions. The sailmaker had his sail loft and the rigger his rigging loft, but for the shipwrights of the shipbuilding yard, paid *per diem*, there was no shelter.

January and February of 1834 are cold, dark, wet months, with crisp, bright days to offer occasional relief from the chill of the winter wind. The changeable Cumbrian weather has a habit of pushing itself to the fore. Some days are 'remarkably fine', some are 'remarkably wet' and others manage to be both at different times. Kelsick writes about constant small rain, misling rain, heavy rain, perpetual rain and rain that falls in torrents.

- Tuesday, January 28th. Wet rainy morning, wind at SW. At 10am the wind suddenly changed to ENE, blowing a heavy gale with torrents of rain. Remarkably cold.
- Friday 30th. A dark morning, strong breezes from the SSW. With perpetual rain and storm in the afternoon, a very hard gale, and thick. Kelsick sitting for his portrait to Mr Pryor.
- Monday, February 10th. Dark morning with showers, wind south. Nothing particular.
- Friday 21st. Strong gales and showery, wind NW. Several vessels came in.

Maryport, c. 1841. Drawn by W. H. Bartlett, engraved by J. C. Armytage. The picture was prepared for William Finden's *The Ports, Harbours, Watering-Places and Coast Scenery of Great Britain* (London: George Virtue, 1842).

Perhaps unsurprisingly given the conditions, Kelsick's health is bothering him. In late February, as attention turns to repair work on the *Saint George*, Kelsick expands on his records of wind direction and postal deliveries with a daily progress report on his cold. When the fine, dry days come, he is ready to appreciate them:

- Sunday, February 2nd. A remarkably fine day, wind South throughout. Got cupped and physicked being unwell. Dined with son John.
- Saturday 22nd. Dark, showery day, wind WNW. Got a very bad cold.
- Sunday 23rd. A remarkably fine day, wind at SW. No letters. Continued clear but cold all day. Still very poorly in a bad cold.
- Monday 24th. Fine, clear, cold day, wind at SW. *Saint George* instructed to be taken upon the slip. No letters this morning. Still a bad cold. Latter part of the day the wind at NW. The *Saint George* taken on the slip.

The final entry comes on Monday, 10 March. Kelsick's diary has lasted a little over two months.

Chapter 3

Once at Sea

A shriek was heard along the shore,
As waters o'er him close;
And where the circling billows boil,

Expiring bubbles rose.
We cannot weep upon thy bier,
Nor strew with flowers thy grave,
But we will steep the leaves in tears,

And cast them on the wave.
No narrow bed entombs him there,
No stone tells where he lies;
His winding-sheet's the boundless sea,
His pall the starry skies.

'The Watery Grave' (extract)

Jonathan Douglas is mining a rich vein of nineteenth-century Gothic imagery with *The Watery Grave*. The poem marks the passing of a young boy swept out to sea. Without the finality of a burial on land, mourners can only send their thoughts and prayers seaward – a fitting metaphor with which to introduce stories of the yard's ships after they leave the shelter of North Harbour and Kelsick's watchful gaze.

The shipwrights of Kelsick Wood & Sons had built these vessels, lived around them as they grew on the stocks and prepared each as best they could for a life at sea, but in the years which followed, their diverse and unpredictable fortunes would lie in the hands of masters, seamen and owners. Many travelled the world's oceans but retained Liverpool, Whitehaven or later Maryport as their registered home ports. Some visited the yard at intervals for maintenance. Others departed, never to return.

There is often no link between the words on the page and Kelsick's pictures, even where both appear to relate to shipyard business. Here, the figurehead design for the *Spaniel* is surrounded by cost calculations for the *Paragon*.

Kelsick's journals make limited mention of the yard's creations after they have sailed from North Harbour but there are many other sources for us to explore. Under the banner Shipping Intelligence, Britain's newspapers printed delayed announcements of ship arrival and departure dates from the world's ports, allowing us to track the progress of each vessel, just as Kelsick would have done 200 years ago.

Other sources add more colour to the ships' stories. Georgian and Victorian newspaper editors had a penchant for human-interest tales which highlighted the extremes of life at sea. Bleak accounts of shipwrecks were a particular favourite, and editors regularly found column inches for heroic rescues or acts of bravery by Britain's seamen. Occasionally, local archives and the nation's museums also reveal their own remarkable collections of official and personal papers.

At the time when onlookers were gathering to cheer the launch of the *Harlequin*, *Collingwood* and the *Paragon*, Britain was in a period of economic volatility. The first half of the nineteenth century brought growth and prosperity but also repeated economic depressions. One came after the end of the long conflict with France and her allies, when the impact of successive bad harvests was exacerbated by Britain's war debts, and another in the 1840s, with poor harvests once more among the causes.

For the country's businessmen, there was reason for optimism. The world lay before them, larger and yet closer than ever before. The American Revolutionary War had meant the loss of important North American territories in 1783 but, remarkably, Britain's colonial reach was still increasing, expanding into what would later be known as the Second British Empire.

The first British settlement of New South Wales came in 1788, and the Canadian territories were of growing significance. A plethora of other colonies in Asia and the West Indies had followed, some ceded from France and others gained through a mixture of commercial enterprise and formal colonisation. The most important of Britain's territories was India, not officially a colony at this time and still under the military and economic control of the East India Company.

Far from being happy, though, Kelsick and Cumberland's other shipbuilders were concerned. There were threats on the horizon, some economic, some technical and others political. Proponents of free trade were vocal and mobilising. The debate about the future of the protectionist Navigation Act would continue throughout Kelsick's lifetime but, from the 1820s onwards, the general direction of government policy was towards relaxation.

Newspaper articles from this period paint an uneven picture of the British shipbuilding industry. Reports of launch days overflow with national pride and magnificence, while other commentators describe the dire state of the industry. When newspapers reported that five or six new vessels were to be launched on a single 'gala day' at Maryport in August 1827, a reader identifying himself simply as 'A CUMBRIAN' wrote to the *Liverpool Albion* with a dose of dour reality.

Kelsick Wood, a self-portrait, with a later hand adding his name to his collar and a pencil note below, 'Above a likeness of K. Wood'. He portrays himself as a man about town, a large and smartly dressed figure at the centre of a busy, busy world of men, women and the occasional cat.

The reporter had been mistaken. Only one vessel of any substance had been launched that particular day and no buyer had yet been found for it:

> It may be presumed that the shipping interest is in a flourishing way in that part, whereas it is quite the reverse; for in these once stirring little ports of Cumberland, a short time ago, they are now in almost ruinous circumstances, for want of profitable employment for their vessels. The building-yards are almost deserted, and the carpenters, many of them, receiving parish relief.[1]

These were troubling times for the builders of wooden sailing ships, but no one seemed to be listening.

A CELEBRATION

The *Cumberland Pacquet* provides a wonderfully candid insight into British national identity when it reports on a birthday dinner held in November 1834 in honour of Humphrey Senhouse, Lord of the Manor and grandson of the town's founder. It is fascinating to step into the world the guests inhabit, their mindset, social conventions and perspective on the state of nation and empire.[2]

As evening arrives, more than a hundred of the 'principal gentlemen' of Maryport assemble in town and walk four abreast towards Netherhall, banners representing commerce and industry held aloft, with a band of musicians and a large crowd of onlookers in company. Senhouse greets them at his sprawling home, and they process together to the Golden Lion, where dinner awaits. Kelsick is to be the chair for the evening's proceedings.

The party take their seats in the crowded, noisy dining room, with the guest of honour seated to Kelsick's right. The *Pacquet* gives a long account of the evening and a near-verbatim record of the speeches, itself an impressive piece of shorthand note-taking. It is a night of fine food and plentiful wine, with numerous toasts and frequent bouts of cheering and laughter. There is a band and several guests sing, including Kelsick, who entertains everyone with an Irish folk song. His son John performs a humorous new composition by Jonathan Douglas for the room, and again when the audience demands an encore.

After a first toast to the king, Kelsick pauses and asks each gent to 'fill a bumper'. With drinks refreshed, he raises a glass to the 'worthy Lord of the Manor' and sets the tone for the evening ahead, 'Gentlemen, I hope that this toast will be drank as it ought to be, and as every thing is done in Maryport, in a manner reflecting credit upon the inhabitants!' The gentlemen do not disappoint. They toast Senhouse with noisy enthusiasm, 'three times three, with an extra cheer'.

Many of the evening's toasts are acknowledged by their subjects, who then pick up the speaker's baton. As the patter of call and response passes around the smoky room, and as the wine and brandy flow, the men speak more freely about their hopes and concerns. A picture emerges as the speeches move between global trade, empire and the nation's wealth and prosperity. To these men, Britain's empire is a benevolent force for good, not only for the country itself but for the benefit of the world as a whole. They see the heart of empire not as military or political, but commercial.

General William Peachy acknowledges a toast to the Army and describes agriculture, shipping and empire as a 'limb of the same trunk'. He then praises the spirit shown by the assembled businessmen and merchants, 'It is this same spirit of enterprise and industry which animates our merchants, and in the times of peace, allows them to waft the precious stores and goodly merchandise of our happy land to regions far remote, extending and promoting the happiness of the whole human race.'

The magistrate William Browne toasts 'The land we live in' in a similar vein. Britain is a land of opportunity, Browne says, and not only for those born into wealth or title but for anyone with determination and resourcefulness:

> there is no man, however humble his station, talents, or desserts, that cannot by a cultivation of his abilities, and a steady perseverance, arrive at even the highest office in the State, and bear over his heart the reward, the bright reward of his country.

His words may not ring entirely true (the guests are gathered to honour the hereditary lord of the manor, after all), but they reflect how the upheaval of the Industrial Revolution was changing British social structures and the rise of the mercantile class.

Browne is a proud Englishman, as he makes clear to his audience:

> Is there any man present who does not feel proud that he is an Englishman… Nay, is there any man in this country who, looking back at the history of the past, will not say that England is not only the proudest but also the best of lands? (Loud cheering.)

When an Irishman heckles him from the back of the room, Browne is quick to correct himself. The country is a land of opportunity for Englishmen of all nationalities, he says, 'When I speak of Englishmen… I of course include Irishmen, and Scotchmen, and in fact all under the same Government.'

The one flat note comes from Kelsick himself. Amid the noisy revelry, Humphrey Senhouse proposes a toast to Kelsick and the good health of the Shipping Interest of Maryport. Kelsick thanks the guest of honour for his kindness but corrects him regarding the health of the town's shipping industry. Things are bad at the moment, very bad:

> As respects the Shipping Interest, I am sorry that I am compelled, in using the language of truth, to say that it was never worse off than now, but we are still cheered on by the hope of better times; and united as we are, Gentlemen, I am sure that Maryport must and will prosper, and that we shall secure it by a long pull, a strong pull, and a pull altogether. (Loud applause.)

William Browne is on hand to lighten the mood and in doing so reminds us that the evening's guest list is entirely male. Browne suggests to the gents assembled at the

Golden Lion that women have a special kind of power, the ability to influence the decisions which men will make:

> We have already drank several interests, the shipping and the coal interest, but I will give you another and infinitely more extensive one:... I mean, Gentlemen, the Petticoat Interest.

Browne's words are met with loud laughter, and he waits for the room to quieten:

> The other day a person came to me in high dudgeon, and wanted my opinion about some grand scheme he had invented for aggrandising the world, but it somehow happened that the ladies of his neighbourhood had taken a very different view of the matter. 'What!' said our gallant hero, 'does the world suppose that I will be put down by petticoats?' I told him that if he were not, he was the only man I ever met with that was not.

The room of gents erupts into renewed laughter, after which Browne brings his gallant hero's story to its conclusion:

> He persisted in his plan, and proceeded in the vain assumption that he would not be put down by petticoats. What was the consequence, think ye? Why, in the twinkling of an eye he was completely annihilated – nay, absolutely put down by an accumulation of petticoats ... And now allow me to hope that every man who struggles with a petticoat will meet the same fate. Permit me, Gentlemen, to give as a toast 'The Ladies of Maryport – Good wives and bonny lasses.' (drank with great enthusiasm)

Of the town's women with occupations listed in the 1841 census, disappointingly few are involved with maritime trades (unless we count innkeepers, of which there are many). There are several confectioners, charwomen, straw-bonnet makers and agricultural labourers, as well as lots of dressmakers and milliners, both sometimes given as a cover for an older profession.

An occasional entry brings us closer to the yard. Deborah Turner of Crosby Street gives her occupation as ropemaker, and Ann Saile as carpenter, although Ann may be referring to her shipwright husband. Elizabeth Sharp describes herself as a ship owner, but even this would not have secured her an invitation to join the gents at Senhouse's birthday party.

Late in the evening, with the dinner and speeches at an end but the wine still flowing, Senhouse announces that he is to depart. Amid light-hearted calls for him to have two birthdays each year, he responds more seriously regarding the planned railway between Carlisle and Maryport. This is far from the first mention of the railway, the benefits of which have been extolled regularly by Kelsick and other speakers during the evening. Senhouse may have felt that he was being played, fed drinks and friendship to get his blessing for this important project. When he confirms that he will indeed support it, many in the room cannot contain their delight.

Senhouse and his party retire to Netherhall and, with his role as chairman completed, Kelsick retakes his seat and the festivities continue late into the night.

twice the lower at the aftermost division
thrice at the upper and ~~twice~~ once the lower
at the midship division for the sum of
breadths - multiply the length, sum of
depths & sum of breadths together and divide
the product by 3,500 for the Tonnage for
Register, multiply the Tonnage so found
by 92.4 - and the product will be the
internal capacity of the Ship in Cubic
feet —

1834

Saturday 22d - dark showery day wind
W.N.W - got a very bad cold -

Sunday 23 - a [illegible] remarkably
fine day wind [illegible] at S.W [illegible]
letters continued [illegible] cold but
a dry - still [illegible] very
poorly [illegible] a
bad cold—

Kelsick has given us many depictions of Maryport's women, such as the two ladies in conversation among his diary entries, but they are harder to locate in the wider narrative of the shipyard.

For all the nation's pride in its empire, economy and innovation, away from the warm glow of the dining room at the Golden Lion, the outlook of characters in this book would no doubt have varied. Such buoyant optimism is likely to have been felt more keenly by more affluent shipowners like William Fisher and Charles Abercrombie, with the promise of profit and fortune offered by the world's markets. Masters like William Scollay and John Monk may also have felt the pull of opportunity.

For the men of the Maryport shipyard, the shipwrights, sawyers and caulkers, each commission for a new ship meant steady work and a reliable, if limited, income. For those on a seaman's meagre pay, however, like Lewis Sinclair or Hugh Murray, facing the world's oceans in these creaking wooden vessels, it may have felt less obvious that being born an Englishman was, as Cecil Rhodes would famously say, to win first prize in the lottery of life.

THE *ELIZA HEYWOOD* (1834): A LESSON IN NEPOTISM

Purchasing a merchant brig was expensive, and ownership of such a vessel lay heavy with risk. Shipping was an extremely dangerous business, and each year an alarming number of merchant vessels were wrecked or lost at sea, often taking their valuable cargo down with them. To spread the financial risk, shipowners commonly chose to hold a smaller stake in several vessels.

The system of ownership had originated earlier in the Georgian era. In typical pre-decimal fashion, each new vessel was divided into sixty-four shares, with a number routinely offered for sale. At intervals, shareholders would review the accounts and hope to divide any profit between them. The *Stirlingshire* (1832) was owned outright by Charles Abercrombie (his holding recorded as 64/64ths), while at the other extreme, the *Archer* (1830) and the *Cockermouth Castle* (1837) each had twenty shareholders.

Registration documents held at The National Archives reveal that shareholders regularly included local townsfolk and business people associated with the yard, ropemakers, sailmakers and so on, or friends and family of the principal owner. This was an enterprise for the whole community. Vessels were built locally by local men, often part-owned by local shareholders, and routinely commanded and crewed by seamen local to the area.

Merchant shipping might seem like a sophisticated investment choice, but for those in a port town in Georgian England, the industry was familiar and perhaps one of the few investment opportunities to be found locally.

The *Cockermouth Castle* makes for interesting detective work, plotting out the relationships between the twenty men, women and even children who appear as investors on her registration document. She was built for her future master, William Bell, under the watchful eye of his uncle, William Fell of Workington, who held nine and five shares respectively. Kelsick's sons John and John Nelson each took four shares as shipbuilder and broker. The remaining forty-two shares were divided between sixteen different investors from all walks of life. The master's brother

Richard Bell invested, as did their widowed mother, Jane. Other shareholders included close neighbours in Cockermouth, clustered around Main Street, among them a banker, a brewer and an attorney.

Six unmarried women held shares. As well as the master's mother, Cockermouth neighbours Mary Satterthwaite and Martha Stubbs each invested, as did Frances and Sarah Denton. The youngest shareholder was still an infant. Mary Oliphant Bell, the niece of William Bell, granddaughter of William Fell and yet to have her second birthday, had two shares in her name.

It is no coincidence that these six women were either widows or spinsters. Unmarried women had similar economic freedoms to men in the Georgian era. Widows like Jane Bell and Martha Stubbs could own property and do with their shares in the *Cockermouth Castle* as they chose. Middle-class widows often gave their occupation in census returns as 'of independent means' or 'annuitant' and occasionally provided more detail. In the 1861 census, Juliana Dawson, widow of Captain James McMinn of the *Campbell*, states her occupation as 'Shipowner'.

For married women, the situation was markedly different and remained so into the Victorian era. Little Mary Oliphant Bell did not wed until she was thirty years old, but on the day of her marriage in 1865, legal ownership of the two shares she held in the *Cockermouth Castle* would typically have transferred to her husband, Thomas Alderson. Property could be sheltered in a trust or identified within a marriage settlement, but a married woman's legal ability to act independently was severely curtailed.

The *Cockermouth Castle* is not the exception. Many of Kelsick Wood & Sons' vessels had at least one female shareholder. Among them, Elizabeth Wilson owned eight shares in the *Wilton Wood*, Elizabeth Harrison held two shares in the *Coeur de Lion* and there were three women among the *James Ray*'s shareholders. Dr Helen Doe explores the surprisingly active role some female shipowners took in managing their investments in her book *Enterprising Women and Shipping in the Nineteenth Century*. Doe calculates that in port communities of the early nineteenth century, women owned upwards of 10 per cent of all available shares.

Just as the profits to be realised from shipping could be substantial, so could the losses, and it was essential that the consortium of shareholders made sure that their investment was in the hands of a dependable ship's master.

Given the near-total control over the ship's affairs that he would have upon sailing from its home port, the chosen master needed not only to be a skilled mariner but also level-headed, sober and prudent with the finances. In a small town and a tight-knit seafaring community, family appointments were common, as one generation of seafarers passed the baton to the next. Such an important position, however, was not one to be influenced unduly by sentiment, a trap which befell Edwin Holwell Heywood Senior.

The tale of Edwin Senior and his son Edwin Junior can be told in remarkable colour due to a chance find in 1959 by an archivist sorting through the dusty files of the long-defunct Whitehaven Joint Stock Bank. The dizzyingly detailed records

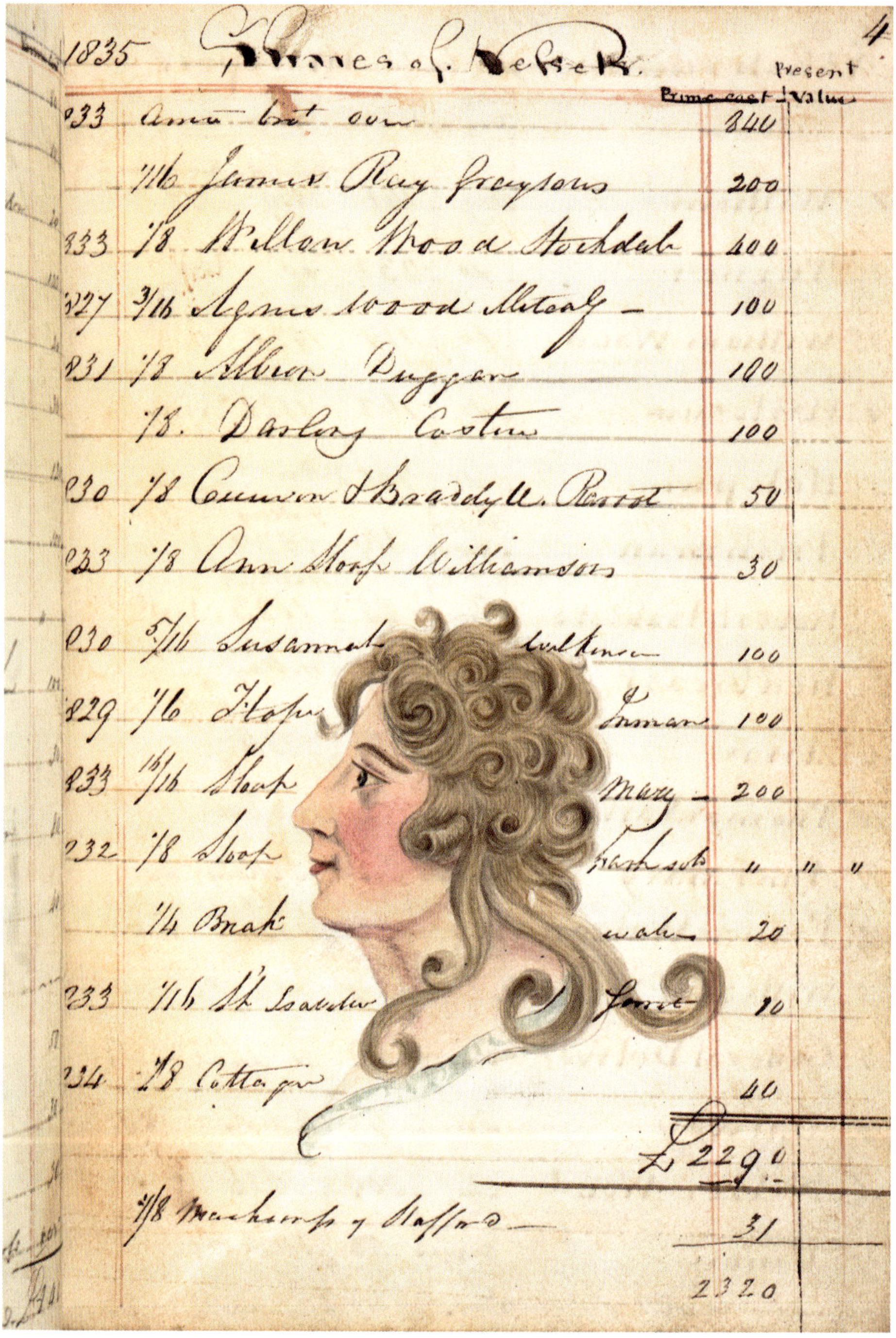

In 1835, in a long list filling two pages, Kelsick wrote out details of the thirty-three vessels in which he held a stake. Shares were sometimes negotiated as part payment for the ships the yard constructed. It was an arrangement that made sense for both client and shipbuilder. It gave Kelsick a diversified portfolio of investments and an ongoing source of income, and it helped to reduce the principal owner's initial outlay.

concerning the *Eliza Heywood* now sit in the Whitehaven Archive and give a glorious view of the pitfalls of an investment in merchant shipping.[3]

A man of greater standing would have been hard to find in the busy town of Whitehaven, where Edwin Senior was not only a solicitor but also the superintendent of police and clerk to the magistrates. The same, unfortunately, could not be said for his son, Edwin Junior. Among the collected papers is a series of letters, written in the years before the *Eliza Heywood* was built but giving a warning of the problems ahead. In each, Edwin Junior charms his doting father with requests for money and apologises for not having paid what he already owes. His excuse each time is the impetuosity of youth:

> I am sorry to inform you that it was not in my power to discharge the whole nor yet one quarter of my debt due to you ... having spent a considerable sum in London, being in company with two other young men, intimate acquaintances ... We very often went beyond the business of discretion for which (being a young man) I plead forgiveness.

Edwin Junior had been in the employ of the Brocklebank shipping firm since 1828, sailing as chief mate on the *Esk*. He had hoped for his own command, but it was increasingly clear that Mr Brocklebank was not about to promote him. By 1831 he was in debt again, looking for an advance from his father on what he hoped to inherit from an uncle, but promising, with his usual charm and faux humility, to mend his ways:

> I have been like many before me idle, extravagant and thoughtless but I now really see into my folly and am determined to act in a different manner if I continue on the path I have followed lately.

In 1833, perhaps hoping that greater responsibility might calm his son's unruly nature, Edwin Senior made a brave decision which led him to Kelsick's door. If his son's current employer would not hand Edwin Junior the command of a ship, then Edwin Senior would purchase one specifically for him.

The *Eliza Heywood* was Edwin Senior's great hope. She was a brig of 226 tons, launched into North Harbour in July 1834. Edwin Senior held a commanding 33/64 share, while Kelsick agreed to take a stake as part of securing the contract. Edwin named his new vessel after his wife, Elizabeth.

Kelsick was in good company as a minority shareholder, and the men who assembled at the first shareholders' meeting represented success in every aspect of Cumberland's maritime business. Kelsick brought shipbuilding expertise, as did William and John Peile. Brothers Robert and Henry Jefferson were wine and spirit merchants, already managing their own sizeable fleet of vessels. Joining them was Kelsick's son John Nelson, a businessman with a solid background in shipping and broking. Edwin Senior brought along with him a fellow solicitor,

Peter Hodgson, and the shareholding was completed by William Mitchell, soon to be secretary to the Maryport & Carlisle Railway Company. Each held four shares apiece, except for Robert Jefferson with three. Between them, the men would have believed that they had the experience, connections and general wherewithal to ensure that the *Eliza Heywood* would be a profitable undertaking, notwithstanding any concerns about Edwin Junior's suitability as master.

Whether the venture arose through wisdom or folly, there is no sign that Edwin Junior's appointment was resisted by Kelsick or the other illustrious shareholders, although his nature would likely have been known to many of them. These men were parents themselves, and they may have felt sympathy for the actions of a despairing father. It would ultimately prove to be an expensive act of faith, however, and the owners of the *Eliza Heywood* would be reminded first-hand why shipping was such a high-risk investment.

With the *Eliza Heywood* launched and preparing for her maiden voyage, Edwin Senior enquired with merchants Crawford Davison & Sons whether they might want to charter her for their West Indies business. There was a delay before the merchants responded, long enough perhaps to make discreet enquiries about Edwin Junior in Whitehaven.

Yes, came the reply from London. Crawford Davison & Sons could use the *Eliza Heywood*, but with the firm stipulation that she be captained by a master of their own choosing. They thought highly of Edwin's son, the letter assured him, although somehow not highly enough to entrust their business to his care. Edwin Senior declined, as he was bound to do, responding that he could not accept an offer which required the *Eliza Heywood* to be 'commanded by any other person than my own son for whom she was expressly built'. The owners made other arrangements, with John Nelson acting as agent to secure the initial cargo.

After the first three voyages to Barbados, Singapore and Valparaíso, Edwin Senior had reason to hope that his investment in his son's rehabilitation was paying off. Each voyage brought a profit and, in September 1837, after the *Eliza Heywood*'s return to Liverpool, the group of owners paid themselves a dividend of £1,300, bringing Kelsick a healthy £81 5*s*. dividend for his 1/16 share.

The fourth voyage showed the first signs of trouble, but that was largely ascribed to problems with a freight customer. A closer examination of the ship's accounts, particularly the expenses incurred at each foreign port, might have revealed a rather different picture, but there appeared to be no need for scrutiny, as everything was going so well.

In fairness to Edwin Junior, there is nothing in the records to confirm a particular weakness, for alcohol, gambling or women, for example. Edwin just spent money generously wherever he thought it needed to be spent, cutting no corners on the size of his crew, their provisions, their time in port or the costs associated with the ship's repair. Through the *Eliza Heywood*, his father had unwittingly given his son

It is likely to have been Kelsick himself who removed half of the page above, as his list of *Eliza Heywood* shareholders neatly fills the part which remains. The page beneath summarises their payments to K. Wood & Sons for her construction. The balance outstanding is £38 12*s*.

the open-ended expense account which Edwin Junior had longed for in his younger years.

Kelsick himself is largely absent from the Whitehaven papers. He attends several shareholders' meetings, but his son John pens most of the yard's letters. John's half-brother, John Nelson, is active first as broker and then as concerned shareholder.

By 1836, the relationship between Edwin Senior and John Nelson was deteriorating, with Edwin Junior inevitably the source of friction. Faced with John Nelson's complaint that Edwin Junior had not called at his Liverpool office as expected, Edwin Senior leapt to his son's defence in distinctly prickly terms, 'I have yet to learn why it should be considered a duty incumbent upon him to dance attendance at the office of or upon Mr J.N. Wood merely because he holds a 16th share of the vessel.'

Stung by even mild criticism of his son, Edwin Senior also lashed out at John Nelson's capabilities as a broker, 'The *Eliza Heywood*'s first charter was through your office and I am sorry to say that "it was no great things", and none of the subsequent offers made to the owners were by any means satisfactory.'

Edwin Junior's final voyage left Liverpool in October 1838. He travelled south to Ascension, east round the Cape of Good Hope and onward into the Indian Ocean. He arrived at Mauritius in February and remained there until June, seemingly in no hurry to leave, before sailing first to Calcutta and then on to Demerara, British Guiana (modern-day Guyana), where he collected a cargo of sugar.

Back in Maryport, the unease among Kelsick and the other shareholders grew stronger as a stream of large bills arrived from each port. The final straw seems to have been a bill from Calcutta for £609 8*s.* 7*d.*, received without the customary letter of explanation from the master. With rising panic at how much the extravagant young Edwin might cost them, the shareholders refused to pay.

It must have pained Edwin Senior to see his son's predicament, but he joined his fellow shareholders in voting to send a more competent master out to Demerara, with power of attorney to remove his own son from his post and to sail their brig home. The owners eventually shelved this drastic, humiliating plan, but a letter shows the depth of Edwin Senior's concerns:

> We are all apprehensive that Capt. Heywood may, if he has been extravagant in his disbursements &c on the present voyage, feel an unwillingness to return to England and meet his owners, and may therefore endeavour to procure a charter to some foreign port, and he may ... render matters worse and worse instead of better. We are all therefore most anxious as I before stated, to see the brig in England, either with or without him.

The *Eliza Heywood* finally arrived back in Liverpool in May 1840. The disgraced Edwin Junior was promptly dismissed as master, and the brig was sold at auction in February 1841, raising £2,200. The proceeds went some way towards clearing the owners' debts, but it would take several months more for an accountant to determine the exact extent of their losses.

Cats and dogs are a common sight in the journals and were presumably so around the yard. Dogs provided security, and cats helped to stop troublesome rats and mice from overrunning the site and nibbling at stores of sailcloth or rope. Kelsick's inclusion of cats in his self-portrait suggests he also considered them as pets. This large tabby appears elsewhere in his pictures, a particular favourite maybe?

Fellow shipowner Joseph Younghusband cast an experienced eye over the accountant's statement. He was clearly alarmed at the general state of record keeping, but was pragmatic as he presented his assessment to the owners' representative:

> The first four voyages show a system of extravagance which I would not tolerate in any vessel over which I had the controls, but some allowance must be made for the circumstances under which Captain Heywood commanded his vessel and he could hardly be expected to sail her as economically as if the Owners had been strangers to him.

Younghusband concluded that Captain Heywood owed the shareholders £1,543 5*s.* 11*d.*, but he placed responsibility firmly at the feet of the owners, who had set no boundaries for their inexperienced young master. A note discovered among the ship's papers, possibly penned in jest by Edwin Junior, appeared to Younghusband to sum up the situation, 'All fair and reasonable disbursements are to be allowed, and allowed too on a liberal scale, as the ship was built by individuals who did not look for much, if any, profit from the concern.' The unwritten subtext of Younghusband's report to the owners was 'Well, what did you expect?'

The dispute rumbled on in the years after the ship's sale. The Whitehaven Joint Stock Bank continued to demand that the owners settle their debt, and they in turn continued to pursue Edwin Junior for their money.

While other shareholders may have cursed their involvement with the young Edwin, his father's devotion remained. In early 1841, as the *Eliza Heywood* was sold and the extensive debts were calculated, Edwin Senior petitioned John Wood for a future post for his son. John responded with admirable politeness, 'I am afraid I shall not be enabled to get Edwin a satisfactory situation soon. Situations are difficult to obtain in this port, however I will do my best for him.'

Much later in life, after both parents had passed away, Edwin Junior retired with his wife to the Isle of Man, where he died in April 1870. No obituary was printed for him but, in 1872, a call for his creditors appeared in English newspapers. Two years after his death, Edwin was still keeping the accountants busy.

THE *FRANCES WATSON* (1825): THE POWER OF THE MASTER

Kelsick was a man of business by the time of his dealings with the Heywood family, his feet planted firmly on land, but he had himself experienced the difficult position of master. He would have known from his own years at sea the challenges which Edwin Junior was likely to face.

It was common for the ship's master to hold shares in his vessel, as it benefited all involved for the man in command to have a commercial imperative. With the weight of his clients' expectations on his shoulders, and perhaps his own share of the profits, it was in the master's interest to make good progress on each voyage. Every day that the crew were on board would cost him and the owners money, but there were some things which could not be controlled.

The voyage from port to port depended in the greatest part on the weather. Losing a week becalmed in the glassy Mediterranean, waiting for a summer's breeze, was hot, frustrating and expensive. A wind in a wrong direction could be equally problematic, leaving masters, owners and freight customers with little choice but to sit tight and wait for conditions to change. It would only be with the rise of steamships that journey times could become more predictable and a stricter timetable demanded.

On arriving at his destination, the master of a merchant ship could find himself waiting outside the dock for several days or more before a berth became free. Arrival could be delayed further if port authorities deemed that the ship and crew should be quarantined. Once docked, cargo had to be unloaded and customs checks completed. The vessel would then be checked over and any repairs made. A stay in a foreign port could be further extended by weeks or even months while the master and agent confirmed cargo and destination for the onward journey. Finally, with crew, cargo, paperwork and provisions in place, the master could prepare to sail.

Kelsick would also have known that the post could be a lonely, friendless position. The first mate was there to share responsibility, but he too was under the master's command. Informality and friendships with a crew could prove counter-productive when an unpopular decision needed to be made. Better sometimes to maintain a degree of distance and authority, as many a teacher can attest.

Seamen did not expect to be friends with the master or even necessarily to like him. What mattered was to be treated with a fair hand. It was a position of great power and great responsibility as, once at sea, there was no higher court and the well-being of the ship's company lay squarely in his hands. A master who treated his men fairly, who ran a tight ship and made good time, would never have trouble finding a crew. At the same time, seamen also learned which masters to avoid: the bullies, rogues and fools, as sometimes circumstance handed authority to men ill-suited to it.

The first few years of service for the *Frances Watson* had passed relatively peacefully since her launch in 1825. She was a brig, but no small coaster for shallow British waters. At 333 tons burthen, she was suited to longer ocean-going voyages and, being a larger vessel, it took a larger crew to sail her. Along with the master, there were a dozen or more seamen, a cook, a ship's boy and a steward.[4]

The *Frances Watson* sailed from Liverpool in June 1828, under the command of Sibson Bragg of Workington. The brig headed south, leaving Europe behind, crossing the equator and sailing down through the South Atlantic. She was bound first for Batavia (modern-day Jakarta) in the Dutch East Indies, from there to Singapore and then back home. Joining the crew on the voyage was a young man called Lewis Sinclair who had signed on in Liverpool as the ship's steward. It was an administrative post, part master's servant and part clerical assistant. As an apparently rather gentle and eccentric individual, it suited

Sinclair well and would give him a small but steady income for the next year or longer.

How Sinclair fared during the first weeks at sea is not recorded, but his situation changed dramatically after an incident with alcohol in Batavia. Whatever had transpired, Bragg was furious. He removed Sinclair from his post as steward and sent him to work as a deckhand. As his crew mates later commented, Sinclair was 'no seaman'. The master's anger did not subside, and Sinclair's inability to perform basic duties on deck gave Bragg frequent opportunity to reprimand him, and with increasing ferocity.

Accounts of the treatment the young Sinclair endured on the voyage are multiple and contradictory. Much of what follows below aligns with the testimony of fore-mast man Hugh Murray, who painted a bleak picture of life under Bragg's command. The resulting court papers are now in The National Archives, and the story was widely covered by Britain's newspapers, including the *Cumberland Pacquet*, its reports being followed closely no doubt by Kelsick and others in Maryport.

Sinclair's health began to deteriorate before the *Frances Watson* reached Singapore in December 1828, where a doctor came on board several times and Sinclair was taken ashore to be bled. There were signs of improvement, but his condition quickly worsened as they began their journey homewards in February 1829. Bragg's hostility grew stronger. The journey to London would take three long months, an eternity on a small, claustrophobic brig when faced with the ire of a spiteful master.

As they passed Java Head, Bragg ordered that his former steward's daily rations should be cut to two pints of water and just one ship's biscuit, with little or no meat, bread or other nourishment. He was doing less work than the others and deserved less food, Bragg reasoned. Other than his one permitted biscuit, Sinclair now depended entirely on what others discreetly passed to him, out of sight of the master, of course. Bragg later disputed this and said that although Sinclair was not given provisions like the rest of the crew, food would be provided if he asked.

There was a limit to the support his crew mates could offer. None of them confronted Bragg directly during the voyage, although, at one point, the master came to blows with Hugh Murray after finding a stash of biscuit pieces in Sinclair's chest.

Sinclair did his best to stay out of the master's way, but there was nowhere to hide. The slightest misdemeanour could lead to a flogging with either a rope's end, a birch or a stocking full of wet sand. The mistreatment grew worse as England drew nearer. Sinclair's mental state declined and his crew mates described him as increasingly wild and deranged. He finally perished while the brig was sailing off the Isles of Scilly, not far from the end of their journey. Bragg found him lying under the ship's boat, handed him a heavy capstan bar and ordered him to stand up and to exercise 'like a soldier with a musket'. When Sinclair croaked, 'I cannot stand upon my feet', Bragg struck him hard about the body. The next day, 13 June, Sinclair staggered onto deck one final time, cried 'Ah! There is the doctor ... calling me' and fell down dead. His bruised and frail body was stitched up in canvas and sent overboard.

With the *Frances Watson* moored off Gravesend, and with no corpse to indicate otherwise, Sibson Bragg went unchallenged when he reported to the quarantine doctor that the steward had died of a liver complaint. Two weeks later, however, somebody had spoken up, and Bragg was arrested in connection with Sinclair's death.

The case was heard first at the Thames Police Office. Several crew members testified as to the appalling abuse Sinclair had received, the most vocal being Hugh Murray. Bragg's defence lawyer suggested that Sinclair had been a 'dull, stupid, obstinate fellow' and likely 'of a diseased constitution before he entered the ship'. The chief magistrate was not convinced. Bail was refused and Bragg was committed to Newgate prison on a charge of murder. He was joined by the chief mate, Peter Miller, who was later released, having no case to answer.

Bragg was smartly dressed when the Lords of the Admiralty convened to hear his case at the Old Bailey on 15 July 1829, with respectable friends in the courtroom. The case for the prosecution rested on the testimony of Murray and his fellow seamen, and Bragg's defence lawyer, Mr Bolland, picked at inconsistencies during his cross-examination. He joked about the floggings with courtroom complicity, likening them to a reprimand from a strict father or a stern headmaster:

> Bolland: Do you suppose that flogging the breech with birch would occasion death?
> Witness: No.
> Bolland: I thought so, because had that been fatal, many of us would have died long ago.
> (Loud laughter, from which their Lordships could not refrain.)

When asked to speculate on the cause of death, each witness gave a slightly different view, that Sinclair's eventual demise was due to either starvation, illness or the repeated beatings all evidence, Bolland said, that his client's culpability could not be proven.

The defence had sown the seed of doubt and, guided by the judge, the jury returned a verdict of Not Guilty, even going so far as to absolve Sibson Bragg of any stain on his character.

The *Frances Watson* was wrecked on the South African coast just six months after Bragg's acquittal. He survived this latest upset, just as he had his trial for murder. He was not so fortunate in 1835, however, and his death came at the hands of another unhappy crew.

Bragg was in command of a schooner carrying pine between Launceston and Hokianga. During a bad-tempered voyage, he was heaved overboard by three disgruntled seamen. Each would later be executed, but as the schooner left Bragg in its wake, one of the three men is reputed to have shouted after him that Bragg should 'pray to God for mercy, for that as he had done to others he must expect to be done by'.[5]

Kelsick equips his shipwright with the tools of his trade, a ruler in his pocket and an axe resting on his shoulder. In contrast to an axe, the blade of an adze was mounted at a right angle to the shaft, which allowed the shipwright to shape and trim the timber as it lay before him. It is common to find Kelsick's characters presented as here, with a decorative curlicue beneath their feet. Although they gain the appearance of a figurehead design, this often seems more like a decorative choice by the artist.

THE *NELSON WOOD* (1826): THE SEAMAN'S PLIGHT

The life of a merchant seaman could be gruelling, relentless and at times immensely dangerous, particularly in rough seas and high winds. Even the most reasonable of masters had little choice but to work their men hard, as a merchant crew could never be more numerous than required, for reasons of cost. It was an inherently hazardous occupation but it could be made far more so by the greedy, negligent or even criminal practices of certain owners, masters and agents.

The brightly painted figureheads and ornately carved sterns can distract from the fact that these elegant wooden ships were working vessels. Brigs like the *Frances Watson* and *Nelson Wood* were built to a budget, worked hard during their lifetime and not expected to last forever. The cherished A1 status assigned to new vessels by Lloyd's Register was proudly displayed on the shipping pages, but once that A1 status had been lost, a vessel could drop quickly through the classifications. With a lower classification, agents could no longer attract such profitable freight and more extensive repairs became uneconomical. Inevitably, not every old ship in poor condition would be taken out of service. Some were sold on to unscrupulous owners, who continued to send them out, secure in the knowledge that they had ample insurance in the event of disaster. British newspapers referred to these ageing vessels as 'coffin ships', often with good reason.

When a ship's company had lost sight of land, they were on their own. Every issue which arose had to be resolved through the crew's combined wits and whatever materials they had to hand, unless by good fortune another vessel happened to pass close by. Many ships and their crews simply disappeared, 'missing, presumed lost', and were never heard from again. Two centuries later, this danger remains, despite the wonders of radio and GPS tracking.

For others, the sea gave up clues as to what may have happened, even if there were no bodies to bury. The *Agnes Wood* (1827), launched shortly after the death of Kelsick's daughter Agnes, had not been heard from since sailing from Limerick on 9 November 1836, after a series of gales along the Pembrokeshire coast.[6] Late in December, a length of keel washed up on Musselwick Sands. With it was the stern of a boat, on which was painted in crisp, white letters on a black background: 'AGNES WOOD • MARYPORT'.

Public and political awareness of the seaman's plight was growing. With each winter's spate of shipwrecks, the calls for change and regulation grew louder. For a brief moment in 1843, the loss of the *Nelson Wood* became the focus of this public dismay, although some of the criticism was the result of misreporting by *The Times*.

The *Nelson Wood* had been built by Kelsick Wood & Sons in 1826, a large brig at 308 tons. Her ill-fated final voyage came seventeen years later. She had sailed from Demerara on 18 October 1843, heading home with a cargo of timber, sugar and

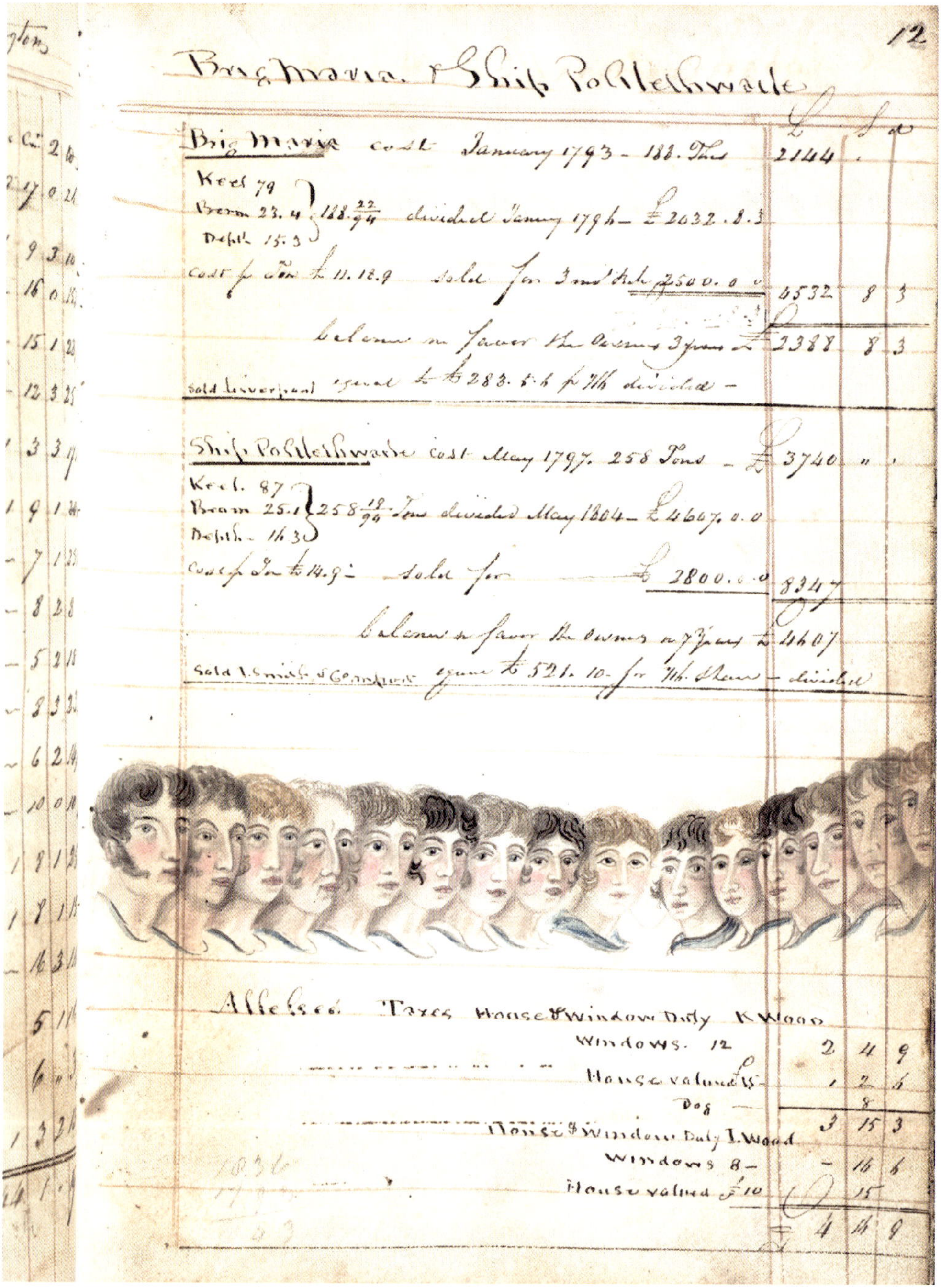
Brig Maria & Ship Postlethwaite 12

Brig Maria cost January 1793 - 188 Tons £ 2144 . .
Keel 79 / Beam 23.4 / Depth 15.3 } 188 22/94 divided Jany 1796 - £ 2032.8.3
cost p Ton £ 11.12.9 sold for 3rd part £ 2500.0.0 4532 8 3
balance in favour the Owners 3 years £ 2388 8 3
sold Liverpool equal £ 283.5.6 p 1/16th divided -

Ship Postlethwaite cost May 1797. 258 Tons £ 3740 . .
Keel 87 / Beam 25.1 / Depth 16.3 } 258 18/94 Tons divided May 1804 - £ 4667.0.0
cost p Ton £ 14.9 - sold for £ 2800.0.0 8347
balance in favour the Owners in 7 years £ 4607
Sold I. Smith & Co. equal £ 521.10 - p 1/16th Share - divided

Assessed Taxes House & Window Duty K Wood
Windows 12 2 4 9
House valued £15 - 1 2 6
Dog - 8
House & Window Duty I. Wood 3 15 3
Windows 8 - - 16 6
House valued £10 15
£ 4 16 9

Kelsick summarises the cost, sale receipt, dividend and profit for the two vessels he had himself commanded, although both had been sold by the family three decades earlier. Below the collection of faces, he has calculated the taxes payable on his own house and that of his son, John. Kelsick is to be taxed for his house, its twelve windows and a dog. His attitude to tax more generally is hinted at elsewhere in his journals. One tax-related page is covered with flies, while on another, Kelsick has drawn a small picture of a man with his trousers round his ankles, defecating.

rum. It had been five months and a journey of some 8,000 nautical miles since the crew had said their goodbyes in Liverpool that May.

The night sky was dark and cloudy on 27 November, and the wind was blowing hard. The master of the *Nelson Wood*, a late replacement at Demerara, later named by newspapers as William Ervin, mistook his position and believed himself to be much further to the south. What Ervin took to be the Bristol Channel was in fact the rocky coast of Connemara, County Galway. He realised his error too late, and the *Nelson Wood* ran aground on the rocks off Mason's Island. Within two hours she had been completely broken up by the sea. Four of the crew, the second mate William Birch, cook Archibald McFerson and two seamen, clung to a piece of wreckage which carried them fortuitously to shore. The bodies of the remaining ten, Ervin among them, washed up along the coast in the days which followed.[7]

Reports of this latest disaster stoked the fires of public debate around the lack of regulation in shipping. The loss of life on the *Nelson Wood* was widely considered to be the result of a familiar cocktail of human error, dangerous business practices and bad luck. Many expressed surprise at the scale of the master's navigational error, but it was the owners, William Robinson of Maryport among them, who bore the brunt of the public's criticism: profit had been put before safety, their vessel had been under-manned and their master inexperienced.

In the case of the *Nelson Wood*, anger at the brig's small crew size was misplaced and arose after *The Times* mistakenly overstated her tonnage. The wider claims levelled against the industry rang true, however. There had been repeated calls to improve regulation of the merchant service through the years, but the state of the industry remained an emotive topic. The press voiced an increasing lack of faith in the industry's ability to regulate itself. A long letter to *The Times* gave a typically damning assessment:

> It is in vain to hope the shipowners will themselves remedy the evil, as their interest is so strong in its continuance. They insure their ship, and sink or swim is all one to them … It is very clear to me … that had the *Nelson (Wood)* been properly manned she would probably have escaped.

The paper's editor shared the writer's dismay and bemoaned 'the ships lost and lives sacrificed to the criminal practice of sending vessels to sea with crews scarcely sufficient to navigate them even in smooth water'.

Public and press outrage at incidents like the wrecking of the *Nelson Wood* did not fall entirely on deaf ears, but 'maritime law is written in blood', as the old saying goes. The path to regulation and safety improvements would be painfully slow, each step coming only after the loss of a great many lives.

In about 1838, Kelsick recorded the fate of the vessels the yard had launched since his arrival two decades earlier. Ten of the first twenty vessels had been either wrecked or sunk. The largest loss was the 333-ton *Frances Watson*, the smallest a schooner named the *Widow's Friend*, at just 54 tons.

THE *CAMPBELL* (1837): A MERCHANT'S MIXED FORTUNES

The travel writer Richard Ayton found little to praise when he visited Maryport in 1814. Having first described the streets behind Kelsick's yard as wretched and filthy, Ayton turned his critical eye to the harbour:

> The harbour of Maryport is very small, and ill-suited to the wealth and commercial importance of the place. The channel is so narrow in parts, that two vessels can scarcely lie in it abreast.

The wooden breakwaters at the harbour's entrance were inadequate, with visible gaps and fractures, he added, and despite the town's growing success and impassioned entreaties from shipowners, the lord of the manor had so far resisted calls for improvement. Ayton admitted this was unconfirmed gossip but then still included it in his published travel journals.

Given the state of its narrow, shallow harbour, Maryport's rise was taking some observers by surprise. In 1821, the *Cumberland Pacquet* contrasted the town's fortunes with those of Workington, where coal exports were declining and rents falling. 'While Workington is in this state of decay, the neighbouring town of Maryport (which, but the other day, was an insignificant village) is as rapidly rising.'

The upwards trajectory continued into the 1830s, as the young town sought to better organise its operations. The Maryport Harbour Act of 1833 established a board of trustees to oversee the preserving and improvement of the harbour and town. The majority of its members were elected, and it marked an important loosening of control by the Senhouse family. Kelsick was named twice in the Act, although parliamentary agents managed to misspell his name both times, first as Keldrick and then Kelick.[8]

In the years which followed, an ambitious programme of work brought the town its own harbour office, custom house and the right to process ship registrations. The physical infrastructure was also developing, notably the creation of a new, larger dock to accommodate many more vessels. No longer could seamen from Workington and Whitehaven scoff that Maryport's narrow harbour was a 'gutter'.

It was a time of optimism for many in Maryport, although not for the town's shipbuilders. Whenever excitable compliments were paid to the industry's health, the Wood family were quick to set the record straight. The industry was not thriving, they said, time and again. Behind the splendour and fanfare of each ship's launch lay an industry in transition. Not only were Kelsick Wood & Sons building an increasing number of their vessels speculatively, they were also facing increased foreign competition, unsupportive government policy and the alarming direction of technical innovation.

The mood in Maryport more generally was on a distinctly upward curve. In 1834, the *Cumberland Pacquet* devoted a large part of its 2 December edition to the town. Ahead of the boozy dinner to celebrate Humphrey Senhouse's birthday, the *Pacquet*'s visiting reporter took a walk through the town and wrote with generosity about what he saw. Rome was not built in a day, he reminded readers, but look at what the 'spirited and populous town of Maryport' had achieved within just a hundred years.

The new drawbridge across the Ellen was an 'excellent convenience' and the reporter was similarly enamoured with the market square. Excavation of a large man-made basin opposite North Harbour, to be known as the New Dock, was proceeding rapidly, he noted, the land chosen being entirely of sand, and the exciting subject of the proposed railway merited an article of its own at a later date.

The most recent innovation was the arrival of street lighting. Until this time, Maryport's streets had been in total darkness after nightfall, save for the light of the moon and stars, and the flicker of candles in windows. But no more. The town was to be lit, and not by the gloomy glow of oil lamps but by the bright, modern dazzle of gas. The first lighting had been timed to coincide with Senhouse's birthday. At three o'clock in the afternoon, as daylight faded, the lamp-lighter began his rounds. Children cheered as he brought his torch to the first gas nozzle and then joined him on his route, running ahead and surrounding him with 'uproarious shouts' as he moved from lamp to lamp and transformed the streets from darkness to near daylight.

Jonathan Douglas mentions the gas lights in a comedic poem, which he prepared for that evening's grand dinner:

> The Stars may go out, and the Moon if she please,
> May change to a pumpkin, or turn to green cheese,
> Since we have created a light of our own,
> To beacon the harbour and illumin the town.

Like much in Georgian Britain, Maryport's development was driven forward by local boards of trustees, subscription lists and unilateral acts of benevolence. It fell to men like Kelsick Wood and Joseph Huddleston to push through the changes which would shape the town's future. The fortunes of less-influential residents lay in their hands, not only in the employment they could offer but also through the energy with which they championed local improvements, initiatives and causes.

The official opening of the New Dock on Tuesday 10 January 1837 was covered in detail by the *Cumberland Pacquet*. The occasion was timed to coincide with the launch of the *Campbell*, the second vessel Kelsick had built for the Dawson family, two years after delivery of the *Paragon*. Among the shareholders was her future master, James McMinn, a Scottish mariner who had recently married Juliana, George Dawson's niece.[9]

The *Campbell*'s launch placed Kelsick and his yard firmly at the centre of proceedings. To heighten the visual impact, the yard's workers had already brought the new brig's masts into position. It risked affecting the top-heavy vessel's stability at this critical moment but allowed colourful flags to be hung throughout her rigging. The organisers were lucky with the January weather and a large crowd gathered. After a smooth launch into North Harbour, the *Campbell* was led with fanfare across the Ellen and into New Dock. Cannons fired and the band on board played 'The Campbells Are Coming' as the brig first entered the large basin and then 'God save the King' when she was safely moored.

The young William Russell was among the crowd cheering not only the spectacle of the launch but also the promise of a bright future for the town. Sixty years later, he recalled the occasion with impressive clarity and mentioned the dock's informal name, Gambles Dock, a corruption of *Campbell*, the first vessel to enter it.

Launches into North Harbour did not always run so smoothly. For the assembled onlookers, the splendour of a launch day was enjoyable, of course, but there was always the chance of witnessing something unplanned. Late the following year, on the day the *Martha* was launched, the tide at Maryport was low and the harbour was especially muddy. As the new brig slid into the water, a log being used to assist with the launch became snagged in the mud, tipping her unceremoniously to one side, where she remained for a couple of hours until she could be righted and moored, undamaged. After all the ceremony and anticipation, it was a disappointment for Kelsick and the owner, John Archer, looking upon the *Martha* as she lay in the water 'on beam ends', an ignominious debut for a vessel intended to face the waves of the Atlantic.

Proximity to a good-sized body of water might seem like a prerequisite for any launch, but this was not an option for the town's shipbuilders further up the Ellen. The Ritson and Peat yards finessed a different technique and launched their larger vessels broadside into the narrow river. It became a source of delight for spectators. A broadside launch could only take place at high tide, and if the right tide was at night time, then so was the launch. A grassy bank opposite Ritson's yard allowed spectators to be involved in the action. As a hull hit the Ellen side-on, it would push a large surge of water high up the slope opposite. Those braver, more foolhardy spectators further down the bank risked being drenched or swept off their feet.

Others chose to build vessels away from the water entirely. The *Carlisle Patriot* reported with delight on the 'extraordinary launch' of the *Lord Ellenborough* in January 1824, extraordinary because she had been built a mile inland. Fine for a rowboat or a small sailing skiff, but the *Lord Ellenborough* was larger, built by Mr J. Haston for the coal trade and with a 30-ton capacity. The men of the yard led her on a cart across six bumpy fields and down half a mile of road, in company with musicians and laughing onlookers who gave a loud and generous 'huzzah!' when she was finally launched into Maryport harbour that evening.

History is littered with stories of launches gone awry and not all incidents in the nineteenth century were as benign as that which befell the *Martha*. In Portsmouth in September 1825, the gates of a dry dock collapsed before the launch of the *Princess*

Kelsick's love of swirls and curlicues is a constant throughout his drawings, and he sometimes integrated them into his characters' features, as he has here with the man's hair. They allowed him to combine the classical elements of his ships' ornamentation with the satisfaction of a well-executed doodle.

Charlotte. As a result, 150 people were sent tumbling into the water from a walkway above, leaving at least sixteen dead. The death toll was higher in 1883 when the SS *Daphne* toppled over during her launch into the Clyde; 127 people died, mostly yard workers preparing to complete her fitting-out once on the water. It remains one of Scotland's worst maritime disasters. In 1898, large crowds gathered at Blackwall to witness the launch of HMS *Albion* into the Thames. At least thirty-four people were swept to their deaths when the stern of the warship threw up a huge wave as it hit the water. An early cinematographer captured the launch and the aftermath of the disaster on film.

The urge to mess with well-laid plans appears to be part of the human condition. In Hull in July 1854, officials tried in vain to keep the boisterous crowd at a distance ahead of the launch of the *Dowthorpe* but, by the time the last wedges were knocked away, there were at least 300 people on board, all looking forward to the ride. As the press reported events, the crowd 'commenced *sallying* her – that is rushing from side to side, to make her rock in the water'. A rope intended to slow the *Dowthorpe*'s progress broke under the strain, and large numbers were thrown into the water, four of whom died, all young men.[10]

The business interests of George Dawson, owner of the *Paragon* (1835) and shareholder in the *Campbell* (1837), lay principally in sugar. With his nephew John, George ran an import business between the West Indies and Whitehaven, and his ships arrived at the Cumberland port with their cargo of molasses-rich raw sugar several times each year.

John rose to sole proprietor of the business on George's death in 1838, as the principal beneficiary of his late uncle's estate. This handed him the sugar import business, with its warehouses, offices and land in Antigua, along with the shares in ships such as the *Paragon* and the *Campbell*. There were also the Cumberland estates of Blennerhasset and Bothel, and the rent he collected on their cottages and farmland would supplement his sugar-trading income nicely. John was now a wealthy man, but in the fickle world of commodities trading, darker days were to follow.[11]

John continued to run the business as his uncle had taught him, but while the nation's consumption of sugar almost doubled between the 1830s and 1850s, the sale price at Britain's markets almost halved, as global production increased to meet demand. Prices fluctuated hugely and a trader buying at source in Antigua or Jamaica could find himself out of pocket at Whitehaven several months later but facing the same fixed costs. To make things worse, the town's sugar industry was in decline. Whitehaven's last sugarhouse had shut its doors in the mid-1830s, and Dawson's clients now had to take their sugar elsewhere to be refined, likely to Liverpool.

On the advertised date of each sale, John Dawson's customers drew lots from a hat and entered his Whitehaven warehouse one at a time to place their orders. He gave a discount for cash but also accepted credit, payable within a generous ninety days. Vulnerable to his clients' own uncertain fortunes, John was one of the principal creditors when Dickinson Burkett went bankrupt in 1845. Left chasing shadows for the money he was owed, John arranged a mortgage of £8,000 against his safe but unexciting Blennerhasset estate.[12]

As a man with a curious mind, sociable demeanour and creative nature, Kelsick's record-keeping can be uneven. He dives deep into some projects but touches on others only superficially. It may have fallen to the unnamed gentleman here, a quill between his delicate fingers, to maintain more rigorous records of the yard's income, outgoings, employees, salaries, contracts and other humdrum matters.

Sugar prices continued to tumble and John's debt to the Bank of Whitehaven continued to grow. A second mortgage followed in 1854 to fund his struggling business activities. Another customer's collapse in 1858 added to his problems.

Bankruptcy can be contagious. John's own downfall came not long after, when the Bank of Whitehaven withdrew its support and called in his sizeable debts. The *Whitehaven News* announced the 'monetary suspension of Mr John Dawson', adding that the 'event has created considerable sensation in the mercantile world at Liverpool and elsewhere'. The *Lyttleton Times* was more succinct, 'Mr John Dawson, of Whitehaven, has failed.'[13]

By March 1859, trustees had been appointed. John was reduced to bystander as his assets in Britain and overseas were sold to remunerate his creditors. He was left with little more than his memories, among them the launch of the *Campbell* twenty years earlier, watching with his uncle, sister and brother-in-law, as their new brig slid into North Harbour to a chorus of music and cheers.

THE *COCKERMOUTH CASTLE* (1837): THE JOURNEY TO EMANCIPATION

British attitudes towards slavery hardened during the late Georgian era, as the voices of anti-slavery campaigners grew steadily louder and more organised. Early success came in the year after Kelsick's birth, with Lord Mansfield's landmark ruling in 1772 in the case of *Somerset vs Stewart*.

James Somerset was an African who had been brought to London by Charles Stewart who had bought him in Virginia. When Somerset later refused to serve, he was forced aboard a ship on Stewart's instruction, where he waited to be transported to Jamaica and sold once more.

Anti-slavery campaigners brought his case before the Court of King's Bench, Westminster. The legal question was not whether Stewart had the right to sell Somerset, but whether the ship's captain had the right to detain him. Mansfield ruled that Somerset should be released, declaring that he was a servant, not a chattel, and was entitled to certain legal rights of his own.

Campaigners pressed on with their efforts. The Society for the Abolition of the Slave Trade was established in 1787 and, two years later, William Wilberforce introduced the first of many anti-slavery motions in Parliament. Eloquent first-hand accounts of freed men, such as Olaudah Equiano and Ottobah Cugoano, helped to make real what had previously existed in the abstract, a practice thousands of miles removed from the everyday struggles of life in Britain.

Their combined efforts resulted in the Slave Trade Act of 1807, a progressive Act which banned British involvement in the transatlantic slave trade. The Royal Navy's West Africa Squadron enforced it as best it was able, but its success was limited by the size of the Atlantic Ocean and the reliance on treaties with other European slave-trading nations. Legally, however, the country's relationship with slavery was still in flux.

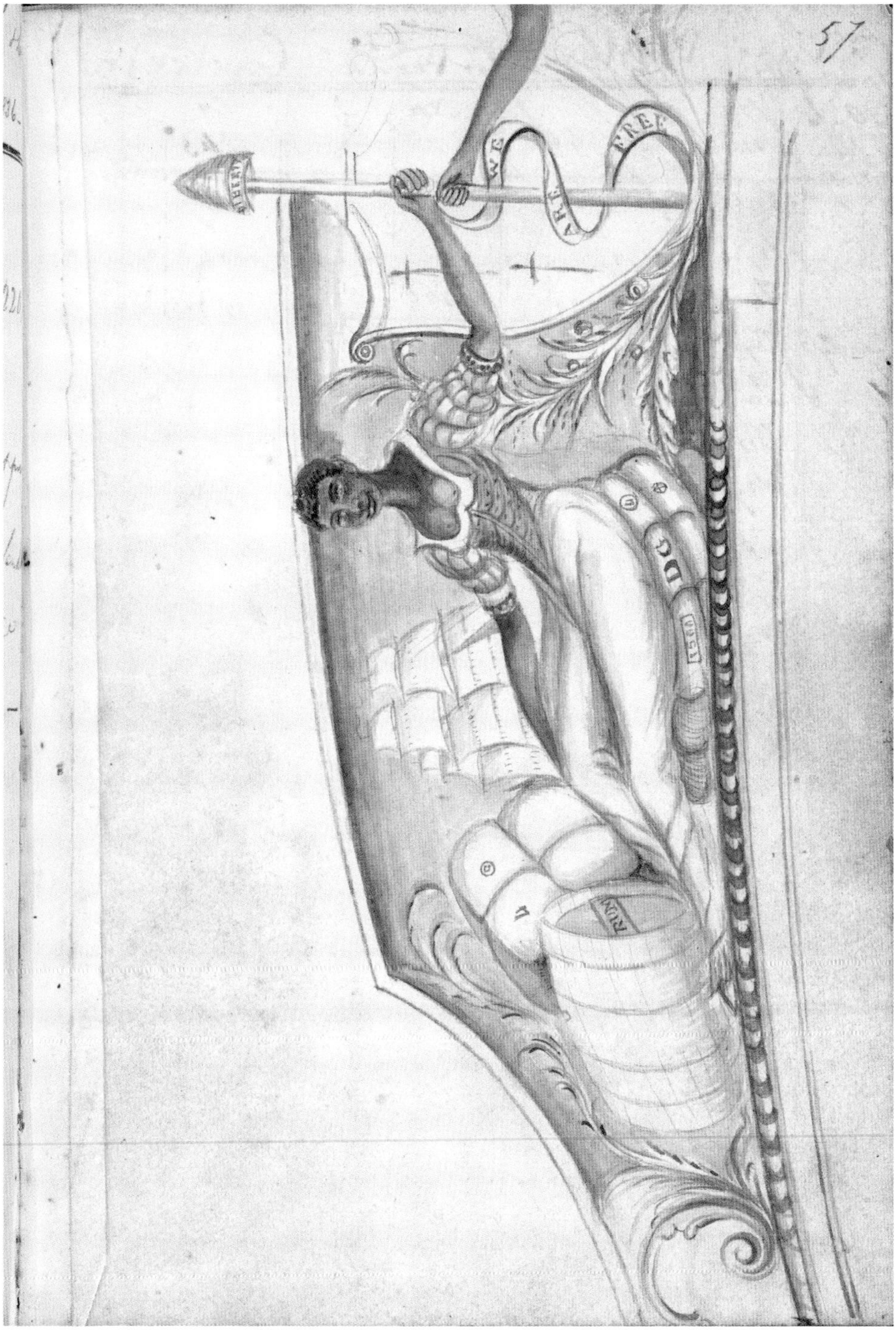

In Kelsick's taff-rail design a dark-skinned woman reclines before a backdrop of barrels and rope. She is holding a rod topped with a Phrygian cap, decorated with the word LIBERTY, while WE ARE FREE coils downwards on a ribbon from her hand. The picture likely dates from shortly after the passing into law of the Slavery Abolition Act of 1833.

The 1807 Act had banned the trading and transportation of slaves within the British Empire, but it was another twenty-six years before Britain banned the institution of slavery itself. The Slavery Abolition Act of 1833 began the process of liberating more than 800,000 enslaved men, women and children across the British Empire, mostly in the Caribbean.[14]

Kelsick drew several pictures marking the passing into law of the 1833 Act, but his apparent delight at the end of slavery was premature, although he may not have known it. Four years later, when William Bell sailed the *Cockermouth Castle* into Demerara, British Guiana, to receive a cargo of sugar and rum in December 1838, the abolition which Kelsick had celebrated had reached its conclusion only months earlier. Implementation of the Act of 1833 had been phased to allow plantation owners to secure a future labour supply. Those held as slaves found themselves as paid but indentured 'apprentices' for the next four years until finally granted their freedom in 1838. The Act also compensated owners for their loss. In British Guiana alone, slave owners received £4 million by way of compensation. The colony's 85,000 formerly enslaved workers received nothing.

Kelsick's pictures may point to his support for the abolition of slavery, but the reality of the Georgian era is that nothing is quite so straightforward. Several of the yard's vessels routinely transported cargos of plantation crops from the West Indies and the Americas, at a time when the majority of the sugar, tobacco and cotton consumed in Europe was produced using enslaved labour.

There were also closer ties to slavery among certain of the yard's clients. John Bolton of Liverpool, who bought the *Mary* in 1833, had been either sole or joint backer of seventy-three slave-trading voyages from Liverpool before the British ban in 1807. Three decades later, at the time of his dealings with Kelsick Wood & Sons, he remained the absentee owner of the Waterloo Estate plantation in Demerara. When the Slavery Abolition Act became law, Bolton claimed more than £35,000 as compensation for the loss of 783 enslaved workers.[15]

The same set of compensation records are a reminder that the use of enslaved labour was not limited to plantation owners. George Dawson, Whitehaven sugar merchant and principal owner of the *Paragon*, was compensated for the loss of two domestic servants in Antigua, Jenny and Joanna, possibly mother and daughter. The young Joanna had been born into slavery. She appears as a girl of just two years old in a register from 1817, along with Joe, William and Otto, all of whom had died or been sold by the time of Dawson's claim.

THE *COEUR DE LION* (1834): THE PERILS OF ASSISTING A STRICKEN VESSEL

The dangers faced by masters and crew lay not only far out at sea. Indeed, shallow, coastal waters could be far more hazardous than the deep ocean. Each time news arrived of another maritime disaster in the Solway Firth, Kelsick added it to his list. His most common entry was that a vessel had been upset. Too light a vessel was vulnerable to capsize, and if too heavy, it sat dangerously low in the water. Submerged rocks were an obvious hazard, but even running aground at low tide on a seemingly benign sand bank could put a dangerous strain on a fully laden hull.

Some vessels were wrecked due to navigational errors. Masters often had to sail through unfamiliar coastal waters, armed only with inadequate charts. A pilot might be available to guide a vessel to safety but masters sometimes chose to avoid the expense.

Others were lost through storms and rough seas. Timber which would last a century or longer when used on land could be weakened at sea in a matter of years and, as a vessel aged, so the risks grew. The movement of the sea would cause the planking of a wooden hull to twist and turn and slowly move apart, faster in rough conditions. Elsewhere, a small fire could spread quickly through a wooden hull as it felt its way towards a flammable cargo of cotton or coal.

The wrecking of the *Coeur de Lion* in 1837 illustrates not only the dangers faced by the crew but also the sometimes-deadly risks taken by the brave men who came to a stricken vessel's assistance. Three years after her launch into North Harbour, the *Coeur de Lion* was beginning the long voyage from Liverpool to Montreal. Her journey had barely begun, however, when she was hit by a gale in the Irish Sea during the night of Sunday 10 September. In the darkness, the savage winds and waves carried her onto the rocks of Dundrum Bay.[16]

The force of the wind had lessened as the skies lightened the following morning. Local inhabitants gathered and looked out towards the vessel in distress. She was less than a quarter of a mile from shore, close enough that they could see some of the crew perched in the rigging. The skies might be clearer, but the sea was still raging, the waves strong and deep after the storm. A rescue attempt appeared hopeless.

A short way around the bay, at the lifeboat station at St John's Point, the local Justice of the Peace, Mr Browne, felt otherwise. The station's regular crew were at the local herring fishery but, with Browne's encouragement, four men of the coastguard took their place, along with two of Browne's labouring servants and the chief officer of the coastguard. The decision to attempt a rescue might have been different if the regular crew had been around, men familiar with the limitations of their boat and perhaps better acquainted with the hazards of the bay.

To leave the solid certainty of firm ground and head out into a stormy sea has always been a brave and testing thing to do. In 1838, these men were especially vulnerable. It would still be another sixteen years before the invention of the cork life jacket, and theirs was a large, open rowboat, without the self-righting innovations which would be introduced later in the century.

The makeshift lifeboat crew handed their pocket watches to their loved ones with a last, nervous hug, and set out on what promised to be a cold and potentially deadly rescue attempt. They rowed for about an hour through the heavy sea, only for their boat to capsize on the final approach. To their good fortune, however, Captain Robinson of the *Coeur de Lion* had ordered his crew to cut away her fore and main masts to protect her hull, and the lifeboatmen were now able to pull their way on board through the tangle of masts, spars and rigging which lay in the water around the ship.

Encouraged by the lifeboat's early progress and maybe feeling that a rescue could be effected after all, two local boats from Clanmaghery also made for the *Coeur de Lion*. One got into trouble and returned to shore, but the other reached the stricken ship. Heavy with rescued men and sitting low in the water, the boat's crew embarked on the perilous journey back to shore, only for fresh disaster to strike when she too capsized. Amid the chaos, the crew of a third local boat, led by John Hogg of Rathmullan, pulled every man they could reach out of the water. Delivering their grateful cargo to land, Hogg and his men returned to the *Coeur de Lion* and rescued more of the crew, before making a third visit, despite the pleas of his anxious relatives. He returned safely once again but with his boat half full of water.

By the end of the rescue, seven men were dead. Five of the *Coeur de Lion*'s crew had perished in the capsized boat, along with two local men, George Starkey and Patrick McGoolaghan.

Six of the seven bodies were found in the days which followed. Funds were gathered for the widow and children of 'poor McGoolaghan', his large family now stripped of its husband, father and breadwinner. Further payments followed, including a pledge of £25 from Lloyd's to the crews of the three boats involved, and £10 to the surviving relatives of the two deceased landsmen. Irish newspapers used the disaster to call for the construction of a lighthouse at St John's Point, the *Recorder* reporting that one local resident could recall twenty-three shipwrecks in the area. It took another two years to be approved, but the St John's Point Lighthouse finally began to operate in 1844.

The morning after the rescue, with the sea calmer and the tide lower, Leonard Watson, the local agent from Lloyd's, boarded the wreck of the *Coeur de Lion*. He wrote to the owners, Fisher & Co. in Liverpool, and described the devastation. The vessel was nearly submerged at high tide, he said, but some of her cargo might be saved if the weather moderated. The *Newry Telegraph* reported the deaths of the two local men with the wry observation, 'Had the crew but remained on the wreck, all might have been saved.'

In the final months of 1837, Liverpool's newspapers announced the sale of the *Coeur de Lion*'s water-damaged cargo. Her hold had been full of manufactured items, all ready to be delivered to a Québécois general store or haberdashers, among them caps, bonnets, jewellery, boots, carpets, coats, fabric, soap and timepieces. The sale of salvaged items continued into December and included watch hands, spectacles and thimbles. The *Coeur de Lion* provides a neat case study of British trade in this era. She imported raw materials such as timber from the east coast of Canada and exported an array of high-value goods produced at scale in Britain's factories.[17]

Remarkably, given the extent of her apparent destruction, the *Coeur de Lion* would later be refloated, repaired and readied to sail once more for Quebec the following year.

CARGO

For a small yard in a small town conceived principally to export Cumbrian coal to the Irish market, it is striking how few of Kelsick Wood & Sons' vessels were destined to operate in Britain's coastal waters. There were exceptions, of course, but during Kelsick's years in the town, these coastal vessels were not the yard's principal

Captain Head tucks into his dinner of soup or stew in an attractively decorated tin-glaze pottery bowl. The name beneath the decoration is an unusual addition by Kelsick, who left most of his subjects unidentified and their actions unexplained. Kelsick also used the page as a tally of rents collected in May 1836.

business. Kelsick Wood & Sons were building for foreign trade, vessels working the deep-sea routes to North, South or Central America, the Mediterranean, Africa, Asia and Oceania. As a result, the nature of the cargo carried tends to be broad and varied.

Vessels were small enough that cargo could be sourced with a degree of autonomy by masters, agents and owners, without the corporate infrastructure available to the East India Company and other large operators. The cargo varied according to the owner's business interests, the routes sailed, the relationships held by the agent and the master's negotiating skill as he sought to ensure a profit from the onward leg.

The greater part of Kelsick's clientele were British merchants and brokers, based in Liverpool and Whitehaven, often with an eye on the profitable trading routes with the Americas. Transatlantic routes brought timber from Quebec, rum, sugar and cotton from the West Indies and everything from copper ore to cow hides from South America. Mediterranean traders carried olive oil, barrels of wine, brandy and sherry, and baled goods such as silk and cloth. Ships calling at West African ports routinely returned with hardwoods, palm oil and spices, while those from the Pacific and Indian oceans might arrive at Liverpool with cargos of tea or rice. The dizzying list of imports goes on and includes all manner of perishable goods: citrus fruits and Parmesan cheese from Italy, pineapples from Chile and sultanas and figs from Greece.

THE *STIRLINGSHIRE* (1832): ACCEPTING PASSENGERS

The shipyard's merchant brigs and ships were generally not commissioned with passenger transport as a primary function, but most found room for one or more cabins. Descriptions tended towards the superlative. The *Archer*'s cabins were 'superior', those of the *Trinidad Pacquet* were 'extensive' and the *Bella Marina* promised 'elegant cabin accommodations' ahead of her long voyage from Liverpool to New Zealand in 1844. In practice, berths on many merchant brigs would have been rudimentary, regardless of any grand promises.

For a ship's master, carrying passengers could prove a pleasure or a nuisance, and his enthusiasm may have depended upon whether he believed they would be good company and compliant travellers, content to eat the food provided and to accept conditions on board. They were certainly faster to load on and off than a cargo of wheat or cotton but needed more attention when out at sea. After leaving port, there was a limit to the steps a master could take to address any dissatisfaction.

Some passengers were early tourists. The grand tour of Europe had been an educational and social rite of passage since the seventeenth century. Wealthy young men and some women travelled through the continent, principally the northern Mediterranean countries, to explore classical antiquity and to enrich their minds with the art and architecture of the Renaissance. Italy was a particularly important part of the tour, with visits to Rome, Venice and Naples on many a traveller's itinerary. The long war with France had halted visits to much of Europe but there was now a renewed appetite to see the world, at least those parts deemed sufficiently cultured.

As with all travel of this era, it was a question of balancing different forms of discomfort. Making the long journey by horse and carriage south through France and the Alps was an option, but continental roads were often even bumpier than those in England. An alternative was to secure a berth aboard a merchant brig travelling to the Mediterranean, although this meant accepting certain realities: there would likely be bouts of seasickness, even on the gentler voyages, and the occasional moment of peril, even terror.

Prior to purchasing the *Monk* from Kelsick Wood in 1830, Lieutenant John Monk commanded a similar-sized brig called the *William Black*. A passenger's diary from 1824 gives a colourful first-hand account of the journey south from Liverpool to Leghorn (modern-day Livorno) on the Tuscan coast. The voyage begins with a violent and near-fatal storm in the Irish Sea, in which the master is forced to cut away the sails to prevent the brig from capsizing. Strong winds then speed them down to the rough waters of the Bay of Biscay, infamous among mariners for its large, confused waves.

The drama continues: the ship's cook dies and receives a burial at sea, and a chance encounter with a vessel taking on water leads to a perilous rescue. Sailing onwards, the short, sharp waves of the Mediterranean prove equally unsettling to the traveller's stomach.

The hapless tourist may have wished at times for the safety of a claustrophobic carriage, its wooden wheels bumping slowly along a French road, but the four-week passage by sea brings positives with it too. He sees and sketches dramatic coastlines, he breathes the curative salt air, writes letters, and spends evenings playing cribbage with the master and dining on deck under balmy Mediterranean skies. The voyage by sail proves to be an experience which would furnish the unnamed traveller with a lifetime of stories before he has even set foot on a foreign shore.[18]

Other passengers travelled for different reasons. Some were on business in a world increasingly connected by commerce, while others were emigrants, seeking a better life on foreign shores. From his modern viewpoint in the 1890s, William Russell marvelled at how passenger travel had changed since Kelsick's day:

> An occasional vessel carried passengers from Maryport. At this date there was no large Atlantic Liners sailing neither from the Mersey nor the Clyde, as there is today. What a change. Instead of having a forty-days passage or upwards, it can be made in under six days now.

One of the vessels to which William Russell was referring was the *Donegall*, which sailed from Maryport for Quebec via Belfast each spring during the early 1830s. Captain John Matches commanded her between 1831 and 1833, carrying

235 emigrants on one crossing alone. Although conditions would have been intimate, a large group of his passengers in 1832 co-signed a letter of recommendation which the owners were understandably keen to publish. Not only were the passengers satisfied with their accommodation, they also praised the captain's 'uniform kindness and attention to our comforts'.[19]

In his poem 'On Emigrants sailing to America', Jonathan Douglas walks among the crowd gathered on Maryport's quay on the day the *Donegall* is to sail. He studies the faces of the travellers, each betraying its own measure of hope, sadness and fear. He muses that for some the journey might represent an escape from arrest or 'infamy', but elsewhere sees sadness in the eyes of a traveller who will never again 'revisit the place of his birth, or close up the eyes of a parent in death'.

The seamen sung cheerly, and launched out the yawl,
To lead from her moorings the proud *Donegall*;
That stretched her white canvass o'er ocean to fly,
As an eagle her pinions to float on the sky.

On the quay piled with luggage, I wander alone,
'Mong groups of the strangers, unheeded, unknown;
The contrast of feelings, and passions combin'd,
Depict in the features, what preys on the mind.

For hope is the emigrant's idol and star,
That mocks his approach and allures from afar;
The anchor he leans on through life—and at death,
The vision he follows, at parting with breath.

(extract)

Research often reveals unexpected stories, only loosely related to the topic at hand. The same Captain Matches, so kind and attentive to his passengers on the *Donegall*, had been sailing a similar North American route in October 1823 with a cargo of timber, when a violent storm blew up. Both masts came crashing down and his vessel briefly capsized. The captain and crew of eight strapped themselves to the deck to avoid being swept overboard. By the time the storm had abated and the seas calmed, five men had died.

Matches and his three fellow survivors were in a dire predicament, with little chance of being spotted by another vessel in the vastness of the North Atlantic. Their brig was flooded, both of her boats had been swept away and all food and drinking water had been destroyed. Fearing a slow death by hunger or dehydration, the survivors fed 'upon the carcase of one of their deceased comrades'. As luck would have it, this 'horrid necessity' was not needed. They were picked up by an American schooner just a few days later. It had made sense to plan for the worst, no doubt.[20]

A journey under sail to North America or the Mediterranean in the 1830s might take four to six weeks, but travelling to the southern hemisphere, to India or further south to New South Wales or Van Diemen's Land (modern-day Tasmania), could take as many months.

It would take a certain kind of woman to make a successful marriage with a ship's master, particularly one like William John Scollay (1805–61), master of the *Stirlingshire* (or *Sterlingshire*, as Kelsick sometimes preferred). He was a Scot by birth, from Lerwick on the Shetland Isles, still a young man but already a mariner with experience of longer voyages. He could provide well enough for a wife and their family but, wherever they settled, William would be absent for long periods, for months or even years at a time, much of it in the distant seas south of the equator. It was not uncommon for wives to travel with their husbands, but that became more complicated if they were to start a family.

William Scollay first took command of the *Stirlingshire* in October 1834, two years after her launch from Kelsick's yard, and remained with her for upwards of ten years. William and the *Stirlingshire* were officially advertised as sailing out of Liverpool, but the time spent there would have been limited.

After early voyages to Havana and Calcutta, William took the *Stirlingshire* further south, reaching Sydney via Launceston in August 1836. It was little more than sixty years since Captain James Cook had first explored the eastern coast of New South Wales and less than fifty years since the eleven ships of Britain's 'First Fleet' had arrived in Botany Bay with prisoners for its inaugural Australian penal colony.

William Scollay and the *Stirlingshire* would go on to play their own small role in the development of modern-day Australia but, on arrival in Sydney, his initial experience of the New World was not encouraging. With his brig lying alongside the wharf, William returned from a shore visit to find that thieves had made off with his chest, taking with it his clothes, his writing desk, the ship's papers and a large amount of money, and all while his chief officer slept soundly nearby.[21]

Better news came shortly after, when the *Stirlingshire* was chartered to carry passengers, troops and prisoners south and west to Port Phillip Bay. Among her passengers were three surveyors, led by William Russell, tasked with conducting the first survey of what would become the city of Melbourne. A small unregulated community had sprung up on the shore of the bay late the previous year and, as the settlers began to parcel out the land, the New South Wales government decided to intervene.

The *Stirlingshire* departed Sydney in September 1836 and made slow progress south through rough seas and bad weather. Sydney's newspapers reported 'much annoyance on board' among her passengers but without ever explaining their complaint. It would undoubtedly have been a long and stressful journey for all on board, and William may have had cause to mutter more than once that he could not control the weather.

57

Chain Cables & Anchors of 90 fathoms proportion of do each other

Tons.	Inch	weight of Cable	weight of Anchor
20	1/2	12.0.0	1.1.0
30	9/16	15.0.0	2.0.0
40	5/8	18.0.0	2.2.
55	11/16	21.0.0	3.0.0
70	3/4	24.0.0	4.0.0
85	13/16	29.0.0	5.0.0
100.	7/8	34.0.0	6.0.0
130	15/16	39.0.0	7.2.0
165	1	44.0.0	9.2.0
200	1 1/16	49.0.0	11.2.0
250	1 1/8	54.0.0	14.0.0
320	1 3/16	66.0.0	17.2.0
400	1 1/4	79.	22.0.0
500	1 1/2	91	27.

Rope ordered for No. 30 – from Walton. Wood & Co. Liverpool

Denomination	Fathoms	Inches
M. Shrouds	42	5 1/4
F. Shrouds	38 1/2	5 1/4
F. Stay	7 1/2	7
M. Stay	11	7
M.T.B. Stays / F.T.B. Stays	33	5
M.T. Stay / F.T. Stay	22	5
Top M. Shrouds		
Sundry Rope		

No 30

M. Mast 31. F mast 28.6
Topmasts 22. T.G. masts 13 –
Low Yards 29. T.S. Yards 24
T.G. Yards 15.6 Bowsprit out 20.
...

Rope for No 30 ordered of Walton Wood & Co 29 Aug. 1834
...

With her pink dress and thick black hair, this lady shares her page with notes on chain cables and anchors. Kelsick is calculating the proportions required, dependent on the size of the vessel. The lady is among Kelsick's more elegant creations, and the white ostrich feathers with their blue tips have been executed with some delicacy.

The headstrong Russell was impatient to begin his survey, but after their arrival at Port Phillip Bay, it was a further sixteen days before they could land, and then another three weeks before the brig *Martha* arrived with supplies and horses. Russell busied himself where he could and prepared charts of the immediate area but, by March 1837, he had fallen out with his supervisors and was replaced by the more experienced Robert Hoddle, who later gave his name to Melbourne's city plan, the Hoddle Grid.[22]

As Melbourne grew into a thriving metropolis in the years which followed, Russell remained irritated that his successor had received all the credit. As he pointedly noted in a letter, Hoddle had been able to draw his neat grid of streets and parks directly over the plan which Russell had already prepared. It would, he felt, have been 'a morning's work'.

While Russell and Hoddle were mapping out the future cities of Australia, William Scollay had continued to go about his own business, trading between New Zealand and Tasmania. It had not all been work, though. William had left Liverpool a single man eighteen months earlier but, when he sailed from Sydney for Guam in February 1837, the passengers included a 'Mrs Scollay', his new wife, Maria Carolina Augusta Monro. Maria's father had been offered a parcel of land in a colony of his choosing upon his discharge after the war with France. Her parents, brother and the baby Maria had endured a difficult six-month journey from Britain to Hobart, Tasmania, only for her father to learn that his valuable plot had been given to a different man and to accept a small sum of money instead. A fortune lost, as her brother Henry later lamented.[23]

Maria seems to have been made from resilient stock and was ready for the challenge of life with a far-ranging ship's master. She travelled widely with her husband in the months that followed. After the voyage to Guam came one to Chile and another to Mauritius. William and Maria sailed from Sydney for the last time in May 1838 bound for London, with a cargo of wool and the prospect of a domestic life back in Britain.

They settled in Edinburgh and began to raise a family. In a marriage with a mariner, the sea would never be far away. William continued to sail the oceans, and there are signs that Maria travelled by his side on occasion. Many years later, when their son William Alfred completed his US census return in 1910, he gave his place of birth in 1842 as 'At Sea'.

The pull of the southern hemisphere remained strong. By 1855, William and Maria had emigrated to Auckland, together with their five children, among them an aptly named daughter, Oceania.

A MISCELLANY OF VESSELS

Just like Kelsick's own journals, this account chooses where to linger and when to move on. Many more of the yard's creations have stories to tell, some large, some small, a few of which follow below.

Maryport 55

No.	Vessel	Tons	No.	Vessel	Tons	No.	Vessel	Tons	No.	Vessel	Tons
1819 1	William	141	1826 16	Nelson Wood	309	1831 29	Darling	101	1835 41	Paragon	207
2	Turner	232	17	Union	58	30	Experiment	42	42	Lord Lowther	269
1820 3	Wm Wood	114	1827 18	Skylark	38	1832 31	Stirlingshire	218	43	Polar Star	50
1821 4	Harlequin	162	19	Agnes Wood	91	32	Charlotte	256	1836 44	Chaico	237
5	Hotspur	205	20	Martha	67				45	Cockermouth Castle	222
1822 6	Irishman	69									
7	Robt Isabella	85									
8	Redbreast	29	21	Mermaid	68	33	Widows Friend	84	46	Campbell	203
1824 9	Ann	55	1828 22	Trinidad P.K.	286	1833 34	Mary	306	47	Bella Portena	227
10	Thos Parsons	325	23	Spaniel	83	35	James Ray	233	48	Cheshire Witch	113
11	Ann & Mary	34	1829 24	Collingwood	282	36	Wilton Wood	243			
1825 12	Fras Watson	334	1830 25	Archer	237	1834 37	Coeur de Lion	352			
13	Wm & Mary	34	26	Monk	170	38	Eliza Heywood	226			
14	Gen. Bolivar	143	27	Prowler	109	1835 39	Tomlinson	125			
15	Solway	99	28	Susannah	48	40	Mary Jones	170			

This list of vessels launched by Kelsick at Maryport runs to the spring of 1837.

THE *WIDOW'S FRIEND* (1832)

The curiously named *Widow's Friend* was launched in September 1832, with the *Cumberland Pacquet* mistakenly announcing her as the *Widow Hind*. She was one of the smaller of the yard's vessels, a schooner of just 54 tons burthen, and was intended for coastal rather than foreign trade, being the property of Wexford corn merchants Breen & Devereux. She would never brave icy waves as she rounded the Horn or face hurricane season in the Caribbean but, as many stories in this collection have shown, British coastal waters brought dangers of their own.

The *Widow's Friend* met her first mishap barely two months after her launch, while underway from Wexford to Lancaster in early November 1832. Her cargo of wheat and barley shifted at sea, which tipped her sharply onto her side and threw the master overboard. Rescue was impossible, as 'from the perilous situation in which the vessel was lying, the crew were unable to render the Captain any effectual aid'.[24]

Her final voyage came just a year later in January 1834. She ran aground near Holyhead, Anglesey, while carrying oats and beans from Wexford to Liverpool. Reports declared that her crew had been saved, but with the ominous observation that 'if the weather does not continue calm and moderate she must inevitably go to pieces'.

The short period between her launch and destruction means that the *Widow's Friend* holds the unwanted distinction of being listed by Lloyd's Register for one year only.

THE *THOMAS PARSONS* (1824)

The business of the *Thomas Parsons* embodies the darker side of global trade in the late Georgian era. Launched into North Harbour in 1824, she spent the last years of the decade trading in cotton from the slave plantations of Mississippi and then, for much of the 1830s, sailing to Liverpool from the West African coast with her large hold full of palm oil and elephant tusks, known commercially as 'elephant's teeth'. The numbers hint at the scale of the ivory trade. On one voyage alone, when the *Thomas Parsons* returned to Liverpool in July 1835, she carried 377 tusks.[25]

Ivory was an extremely useful material, dense and smooth, easy to work and unmarked by the pores and vessels common to bone. It was suited to both ornamental items and everyday objects such as handles, piano keys and billiard balls. The dust and shavings were also put to use, appearing in cleaning products and medicine. Mrs Beeton even included a recipe for ivory jelly in her *Book of Household Management*.

The *Thomas Parsons* was commanded by fourteen different captains within the sixteen years of her existence, three of whom died while in her command. Captain Macklin perished in 1833 on a trip from Fernando Po to Liverpool, while Captain Eagles breathed his last two years later at Bonny River, aged just twenty-three. The end for Captain McKinny, the crew and the barque itself came in a huge ball of fire in 1840, while anchored at Old Calabar. Newspapers stated the cause with surprising certainty as a spark from a cigar which someone had foolishly smoked next to the ship's magazine, although how anyone could have known this is rather hard to say.

THE *BLACK PRINCE* (1838)

A settled ship's company was a blessing on any long voyage. The crew would learn the ways of the ship, work together more effectively and generally take up less of the master's time. Conversely, problems with morale or discipline could leave a master facing one staffing crisis after another.

Captain William Greenhalgh of the *Black Prince* (1838) faced his share of such difficulties in 1860. Historian David Burrell examined the brig's voyage for an article to mark the 250th anniversary of Lloyd's List in 1984. Keeping up with the crew movements through Burrell's research is like tackling a school maths problem.[26]

Greenhalgh and the *Black Prince* departed Liverpool for Chile in May 1860 with a crew of thirteen. Among them was the ship's cook, George Robinson, who was to play a large role in setting morale on board. He refused to follow the master's orders and, perhaps more concerningly, proved to be incompetent in his important job. Seamen were poorly paid and worked long and exhausting hours in wet, cold conditions, but much of that could be accepted if the food was hot, tasty and plentiful.

Two men were swept overboard as the *Black Prince* rounded Cape Horn, although one was pulled back to safety. Problems with discipline resurfaced on arrival at Valparaíso. Three of the crew deserted, among them the incompetent cook. To make matters worse, several seamen went ashore without leave, got into trouble and were briefly jailed. Greenhalgh signed up replacements for the dead and deserted men while what remained of his sorry crew nursed their hangovers. He also secured the services of a new cook, who then failed to come on board before they sailed for South Africa.

The master's patience seems finally to have run out in Cape Town, after another attempted desertion. Greenhalgh discharged the entire ship's company, everyone except for three young apprentices. To rebuild his crew from scratch would have been a frustrating and unwelcome task, but there was a lot of sailing still to be done.

The ship's articles listed sixteen men before they sailed for Mauritius. Of these, four failed to come on board and one was quickly put ashore for refusing to work. After this unpromising start, Greenhalgh's recruitment efforts appear to have paid off. Aside from one deserter in Mauritius, the rest of the crew remained together. That is not to say they were happy, rations being the issue once more. The crew complained first about a shortage of sugar, and then once more in Colombo, Ceylon (modern-day Sri Lanka), where provisions were again running low.

Whether or not Greenhalgh finally hired a skilled ship's cook or purchased more food for his men, he completed his voyage as intended. The *Black Prince* sailed into the port of London nine months later, ready to unload her cargo of coffee at West India Dock.

THE *GENERAL GASCOYNE* (1830), THE *SENHOUSE* (1832) AND THE *LORD SANDON* (1832)

Shipbuilding would always be a financially risky undertaking, prone to episodes of boom and bust. With no more than two, occasionally three, new vessels built each year, and limited space for repair work, everything depended on the order book.

A confirmed order for a new ship or brig brought short-term security for the yard's owners, shipwrights and balance sheet.

The *Paragon* represented the yard's preferred way of working, with the comfort of a signed contract and payment schedule in place before time and valuable materials were invested into a project. Yet even a respected shipyard like Kelsick Wood & Sons was vulnerable to gaps in its order book, especially during an economic downturn or in the face of increased competition. As the 1830s arrived, it seemed to be happening with alarming regularity.

Where no client had put their name to a contract, Kelsick had little choice but to begin a build speculatively, at the yard's own expense. It kept his workforce intact and productive during leaner times but left him with the decisions of what to build and where to find a buyer. Each speculative build was a gamble, but sometimes it was the only hand to play.

During a particularly difficult spell between 1830 and 1832, Kelsick turned three times to John Nelson, his well-connected son and Liverpool shipping agent, to seek buyers for the yard's vessels, still unsold as they neared completion. John Nelson placed a series of announcements in *Gore's Advertiser* and the *Liverpool Standard* and described the vessels' many qualities. Each, he stated, could be readied for launch at short notice.

The yard had assigned temporary names to the three vessels while under construction, naming each after a local politician or dignitary. After buyers came forward, the *Senhouse*, *Lord Sandon* and *General Gascoyne* became the *Charlotte*, the *Stirlingshire* and the *Monk*. Kelsick continued the pattern in 1835 with the *Lord Lowther*, renamed the *Alexander* after her launch.

Shipowners, it seems, preferred to name a new vessel in honour of a beloved family member or their home county rather than the local Member of Parliament.

THE *JAMES RAY* (1833)

Alongside reports of deadly shipwrecks, British newspaper editors also found room for smaller, feel-good tales, like that of the parrot of the *James Ray* (1833).[27]

The *James Ray* sprang a leak on a voyage from Trieste to Liverpool in 1852. Seawater soaked the heavy cargo of grain and Captain Lang and his crew of eleven were forced to abandon ship. Crowded into the longboat, armed with chronometer and papers, provisions and a pet parrot, the twelve men set a course for Malta, some 175 miles away, where they arrived safely eight days later. The story appeared as a column filler up and down the country. Lang had done well to lead his men to safety but, for the British press, the seamen and their parrot were the true stars, 'The sailors, with the humane feeling which is often shown, would not allow a parrot to perish, but took it with them, and it is now alive in Malta.'

THE *BELLA PORTENA* (1837)

The docking of the *Bella Portena* at Bridgetown, Barbados, was the cause of some excitement in July 1857 or was certainly presented as such by local retailers. A flurry of advertisements appeared in the *Barbadian* newspaper in the days which followed, as shopkeepers rushed to announce the wide array of items they could now offer to their clientele. The adverts make regular mention of the ship's name and seek to portray her arrival as a newsworthy event.[28]

George Whitfield placed several adverts in quick succession, promoting his new stock of Cumberland hams, potted lobster, stewed veal, ox cheek and a range of preserved mutton dishes.

Barrow & Dummett announced to the island's fashionable ladies that the eagerly awaited silk and straw bonnets were now available and also promoted their perfumes from London's Bond Street.

DP Cotton advertised their supply of cheese ('*ENGLISH CHEESE!!* Both North Wiltshire and Double Gloster'), as well as spiced bacon, sparkling German wine and fifty barrels of Allsop's 'celebrated' pale ale.

This fanfare is not unique to the *Bella Portena*; indeed the arrivals of the *Jessey* and the *Maria* get similar attention during the same month. Each merchant brig was playing its own small part in the increasingly complex web of global trade, a significant part of which passed through the wholesale warehouses in the ports of London and Liverpool.

THE *IRISHMAN* (1822) AND THE *POLAR STAR* (1835)

While the *Stirlingshire* reached Australia and New Zealand, and the *Mary* (1838) and *Eliza Heywood* sailed the Indian Ocean, others were destined to remain closer to home. The *Irishman* (1822) and the *Polar Star* (1835) were both built for service on the Carlisle Ship Canal. The *Polar Star* was an icebreaker, with a thick hull and a single purpose: to keep the cold winter waters of the canal free of ice, so that vessels like the *Irishman*, which plied their trade along its route, could operate through the long, dark months.[29]

Chapter 4
Challenges

No sign of storm was in the sky,
Of danger on the deep;
The sea-weeds floated slowly by,
The fiends of ocean seem'd to lie

On Solway Frith asleep.
But soon the waves began to swell,
By agency unseen;
But why they heave, we cannot tell,
Yet every time they rose and fell,
His little boat was seen;

'Written on the death of
Matthew Brougham' (extract)

Jonathan Douglas records that it was a still, calm day in November 1832 when the eccentric Matthew Brougham set out from Maryport harbour in his fishing boat. Despite the clear conditions, the swell of the sea gathered strength. As the large waves rose and fell, Brougham could be spied from the shore as he struggled in vain to keep his little craft afloat.

During the 1830s, Kelsick Wood & Sons were also battling increasingly strong currents. At a time when businessmen, engineers and the nation's press were marvelling at the wonders of the modern age, the skies were darkening for those industries not able to adapt or compete in this new technological world. With the family business under threat, Kelsick and his sons, like all good custodians, fought to protect their interests. There were changes the yard could make, political causes to be fought and, hopefully, tides to be turned back.

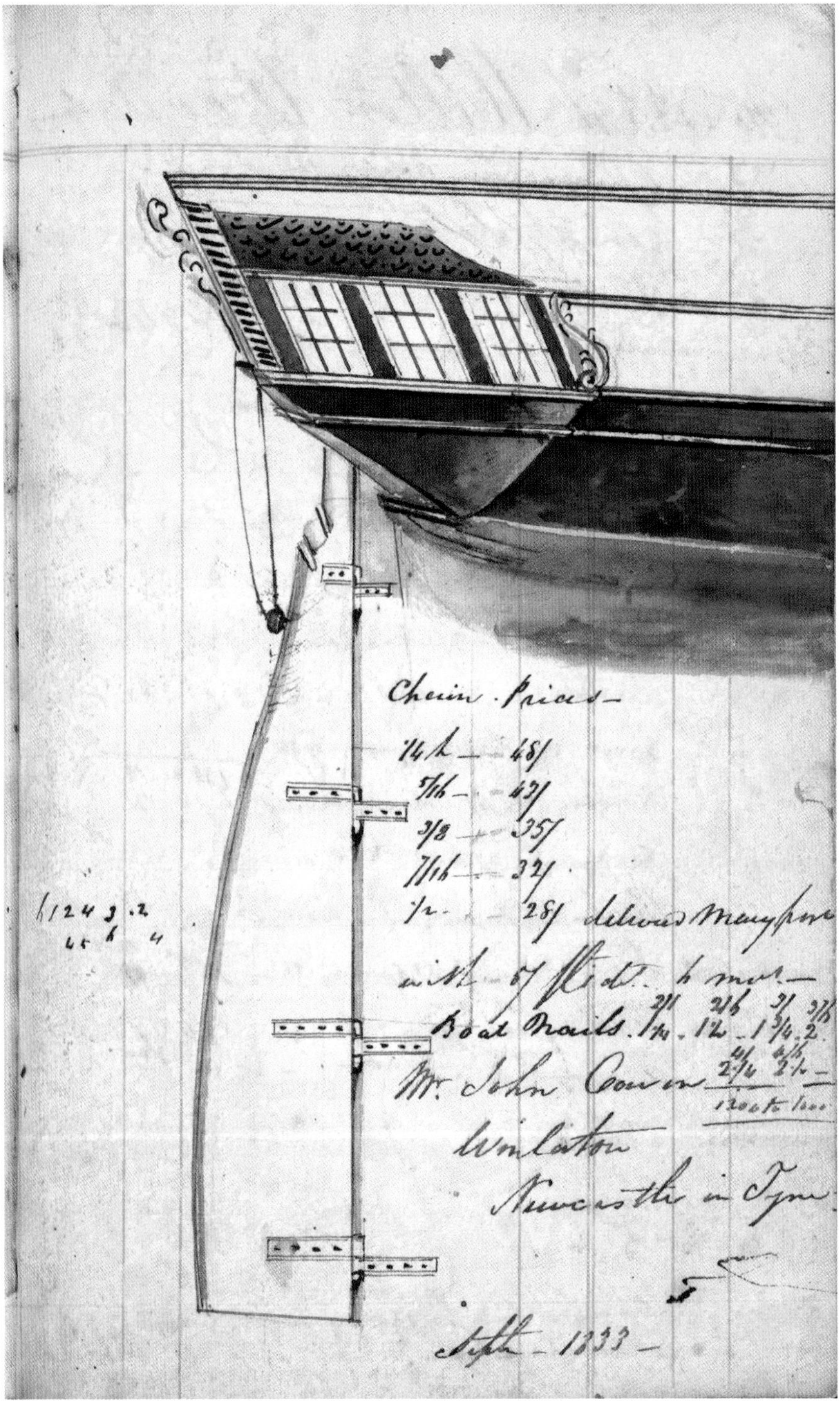

There is no vessel name alongside this picture of a ship's stern and rudder. The costs and calculations appear at first sight to be related to the drawing but instead concern the price of chain and boat nails from John Cowen, a blacksmith in Winlaton, Newcastle upon Tyne.

THE *WILTON WOOD* (1833): THE DANGERS OF FREE TRADE

The public debate about the merits of free trade grew ever more heated during the 1820s and 1830s. Much of the press coverage centred on the protectionist Corn Laws, which served to fix the price of grain, but it was the Navigation Act which was more pertinent to the nation's shipbuilders. Navigation Acts of various hues had existed for centuries, as governments sought to ensure a strong and stable shipping industry. The nature of the Acts ebbed and flowed through the years, as modifications and supplementary Acts strove to keep them relevant.

Supporters of these restrictive Acts argued that the need for a strong national shipbuilding industry had been amply demonstrated during Britain's wars with France. Some industries were too important to leave to chance. Building and equipping the Royal Navy's huge fleet of ships had only been possible due to the depth of skill among the nation's shipbuilders and the size of its domestic merchant fleet.

An array of such policies was still in place in the late Georgian era, although less strict than Kelsick and his fellow shipbuilders might have wished. Only British ships (and others by exception) could import certain goods into the United Kingdom, and many other articles faced additional taxes when arriving in foreign vessels. A wider set of rules governed colonial trade, further favouring British-built vessels. The shipbuilding industry had been one of the main beneficiaries of these policies. Britain's shipbuilders had no monopoly on the construction of merchant brigs, but such arrangements put foreign yards at a distinct disadvantage.

The protectionist Navigation Acts found some surprising allies. The economist and free trade advocate Adam Smith argued vociferously against trade restrictions in his celebrated *Inquiry into the Nature and Causes of the Wealth of Nations* (1776), but made an exception for the shipping industry:

> The defence of Great Britain, for example, depends very much upon the number of its sailors and shipping. The act of navigation, therefore, very properly endeavours to give the sailors and shipping of Great Britain the monopoly of the trade of their own country, in some cases, by absolute prohibitions, and in others by heavy burdens upon the shipping of foreign countries.[1]

Not everyone viewed the Acts in such a positive light. The policies were a complicated frustration for many British merchants and industrialists, among them the owners of Lancashire's thriving cotton mills, which depended on the steady supply of raw materials from the Americas and elsewhere. Each barrier, each bureaucratic hurdle or additional tax, impacted their production costs and the ability to reach export markets. As opposition to the policies grew louder, British governments loosened restrictions and granted exemptions. The nation's shipbuilders had reason to be concerned.

Kelsick's son Wilton addressed the Cumberland County Meeting in Wigton on the subject of free trade in January 1830. He spoke eloquently about how the shipbuilding industry was suffering, a situation made worse by an unsupportive government and a punitive tax regime. Wilton was particularly incensed by changes to allow other nations to trade directly with Britain's colonies. The Navigation Act had been diluted in recent years by 'treaties of reciprocity' with certain nations, Wilton said. He cited Newfoundland, where British merchants were now being undercut by their German rivals. The reasons for the German success were partly economic but also culinary:[2]

> But no wonder the Germans sailed their vessels so cheaply, when the way in which they fed their crews was considered ... horse beans and bacon fat cabbages; and they thought the mess delicious [a laugh]. Would the people of England like to see their hardy tars, the right arm of their strength, fed in this way?

Viewed through Wilton's eyes, and those of his father, the threat from foreign shipyards loomed large. Beyond Britain's shores, there were several countries with extensive shipbuilding operations, all ready to undercut them and put their men out of work. Yards in North America had the advantage of easy access to a seemingly endless supply of low-cost, local timber. By contrast, Kelsick Wood & Sons' costs were inflated by the need to import much of the wood they used, sometimes from thousands of miles away.

These worries were nothing new. When the local press and business owners sought to break the trade unions in 1825, they regularly invoked the spectre of competition. If you don't build these ships, they said, and accept the salaries which the yard owners dictate, there are yards in other countries that will do so. There were rumoured to be thirty to forty large vessels being built in Quebec at that time, mostly intended for the British merchant service. National pride ran high, but if costs and taxes were lower elsewhere, the orders would follow.

British shipbuilders argued that they produced high-quality vessels, using durable hardwoods, whereas North American yards turned more to spruce and other softwoods. Domestic production costs might be high, they said, but you pay for quality.

The threat was not confined solely to the sale of new vessels. Part of a yard's income came from the maintenance work required annually to keep wooden ships seaworthy. In the absence of any protection, owners could send their ships to wherever the work could be undertaken most cheaply or conveniently.

Wilton worried for the future of the family business. Shipbuilders were in a vulnerable position, and he described the impact he was seeing in Cumberland:

> At the present moment there are at least twenty new vessels in this County unsold, and for which the builders are unable to find purchasers. This is the effect of free trade, which is taking

the whole of the carrying business out of the hands of the ship-owners of this country, and placing it in those of foreigners.

The Corn Laws would be repealed in 1846, although only after inflated grain prices contributed to the catastrophic Irish famine. The Navigation Act was repealed three years later. The loss of protection hit British shipyards just as Kelsick and Wilton had feared it would. The impact from Canadian yards was felt most keenly, and between 1843 and 1854, an average of 45 per cent of new tonnage registered in Liverpool was Canadian-built. Over time, the rise of larger, iron-hulled ships brought about a recovery in the health of British shipbuilding more generally, but this would have been of little comfort to small, pre-industrial yards like Kelsick Wood & Sons. It was another nail in their old wooden coffin.

Wilton's bright future was brought to an abrupt and violent end just two years after his speech in Wigton. He was in Whitehaven on the evening of Wednesday 2 May 1832, to meet his younger brother, Kelsick Junior, who was arriving by steamer from Liverpool with a friend, Ralph. After a quick drink, the three young men continued their conversation in the back of the family's carriage, while long-standing servant Edward Marshall, mistakenly named as Spratt in early newspaper reports, sat up front and guided the horse back through the night. As they approached the descent towards Moresby Hall, the horse suddenly took fright and bolted. Marshall fought to keep the speeding wheels on the track but lost control as they reached the foot of the hill. The carriage slammed sideways into the end of a wall.[3]

Kelsick Junior staggered free from the wreckage and raised the alarm at the house of a blacksmith, before collapsing unconscious. The blacksmith and a local doctor hurried to the site of the accident, where a grim scene awaited them. The impact had cut the carriage almost in two, and the remaining occupants had felt its full force. Wilton died from his injuries shortly after the blacksmith first reached him, and Marshall never regained consciousness. Ralph's leg required amputation, while Kelsick Junior needed only rest. The runaway horse was found the following morning, skittish but unharmed.

The coroner's verdict was Accidental Death, but theories soon emerged as to what had spooked the horse, among them flickering fires maintained at a nearby coal mine. The accident cast a gloom over the town and Maryport's small chapel overflowed with mourners for Wilton's funeral on Monday 7 May, where his body was borne to its grave by four shipwrights.

One year later, Kelsick named a vessel in his son's memory. The *Wilton Wood* was a snow of 243 tons, built for William Stockdale & Co. After her launch in September 1833, Kelsick took the unusual step of copying complimentary press reports into his journal. For the *Cumberland Pacquet* to praise the yard's creations was nothing new, but it may indeed be that the yard's craftsmen had given particular care and attention to the vessel which bore Wilton's name. Many of them had mourned his death, and some had carried his coffin.

There is a strong likeness between the several depictions Kelsick drew of his son Wilton, with the same thin face, mess of dark hair and sideburns.

THE *CHESHIRE WITCH* (1837): STEAM

Steam would transform travel on the world's seas just as it would on land, but the revolution came about over several decades.

Forty years after the first steam-powered vessel had been demonstrated, wooden-hulled sailing ships remained dominant for longer ocean-going journeys. Coal was expensive and heavy, and its bulk limited space for cargo. It also had to be loaded into the hold, which could delay departure, and required extensive infrastructure at each port visited. By contrast, wind power was free and sails provided a high degree of independence. There were no fuel bills and no temperamental engines or boilers. Advocates of sail may have thought: why would anyone want to change?

But the technical advances and patent applications kept on coming. Improvements to surface condensers meant that an engine's steam could be recycled and ships needed to carry less water. Screw propellers began to be used in preference to side-mounted paddle wheels. They were more powerful, less prone to damage and functioned well in heavy seas, unlike paddles which were liable to rise out of the water, increasingly so as the coal load lightened. Despite these and other innovations, steamships were still built with masts and carried sails to save precious coal or to bring them home in the event of engine failure.

Freed from the unpredictable influence of the wind, shipping agents' expectations changed. They demanded shorter journey times and more rigid timetables, and with that came increased pressure on masters to meet aggressive targets.

Kelsick and his clients may have looked warily at the competition, as sail and steam were not always happy neighbours. In the close confines of a crowded port, a boiler explosion or a wandering spark from a steamer chimney could spell trouble for a wooden-hulled ship and its sails.

The Royal Navy faced similar decisions about the future of its fleet and was reluctantly accepting the shift in power. When Sir Humphrey Fleming Senhouse acknowledged a toast to 'The wooden walls of old England' at his cousin Humphrey's birthday party in 1834, he gave his thoughts on the future of maritime warfare. Sir Humphrey had been a lieutenant on HMS *Conqueror* at Trafalgar in 1805 and served most recently as captain of the three-decker HMS *St Vincent*. He acknowledged with some sadness that such majestic sailing ships belonged to a bygone age, 'Proud and graceful as our noble seventy-fours are, still one of these little dark steam-vessels, armed with a gun of large calibre, will, I believe, at some future time, destroy those splendid floating castles which in appearance have so much superiority.'

The battle for supremacy was played out in miniature on the shipping pages of *Gore's Liverpool General Advertiser*, where announcements of each ship's expected departure date and destination were accompanied by small silhouettes to indicate whether a vessel was wind- or steam-powered. As the decades of the nineteenth century passed, the little black steamships spread across the page, while the sailing ships dwindled in number.

The commercial exploitation of steam power brought threats and opportunities for the nation's shipbuilders, challenges to which some would rise and others would not. The *Cheshire Witch* was part of Kelsick's response to this shift. She was small by the yard's standards, just 85 feet long and 113 tons burthen, and her hull was unremarkable, built around an oak frame, with elm and red pine planking. What set her apart was that she was an iron-paddle steam ferry, the very first steam vessel to be built by Kelsick Wood & Sons or indeed by any of the Maryport yards.

The order for the *Cheshire Witch* likely came via Kelsick's son, John Nelson, a founding co-director of the Royal Rock Ferry Steam Packet Company. The founders published the prospectus for their new venture in April 1836. Four steamboats would operate a half-hourly service between George's Pier, Liverpool, and the company's newly built wharf at Rock Ferry, Birkenhead. Next to the wharf was a hotel, also part of the company's portfolio, and sufficient land to lay out an expansive pleasure garden, as a further lure to draw visitors to this elegant new suburb across the Mersey.[4]

Birkenhead was no longer a quiet village, isolated at the north-western tip of the Wirral peninsula. The first steam ferry service had begun from Liverpool to Birkenhead at Woodside in 1822, the catalyst for ambitious and continued investment. The Laird family had established their ironworks and shipbuilding businesses there shortly after, and a smart new town centre had been built. Radical developments like trams and a public park were to follow.

It may have taken John Nelson's involvement for his father to embrace the rise of steamships, but Kelsick shows elsewhere that he was not blind to the changing world. He was among the trustees who championed the introduction of gas lighting and other civic improvements during the 1830s and was similarly prominent in the project to bring the steam-powered railway to the town. Whether such bold advances would be possible within the cramped confines of his shipbuilding yard would be a different matter.

The *Cheshire Witch* was news in Cumberland in 1837, but it was the launch of the SS *Great Western* that same year which made the headlines nationally. Built in Bristol by the engineer Isambard Kingdom Brunel, the *Great Western* was, for a brief moment at least, the largest passenger steamship of her day, with two huge paddle wheels for propulsion and equipped with the largest engines yet built, drawing steam from four iron boilers, each with three furnaces. However, like the *Cheshire Witch*, she was wooden-hulled, built of oak by traditional methods.

Another engineering landmark came the following year. Shortly after launching the 694-ton ship *Mary* in 1838, Kelsick copied out the specification of the steamer SS *British Queen*, 'the largest vessel in the world' at 1,862 tons. Her engines could generate 500 horsepower, but all that power came at a cost. Kelsick noted that the

There are not many full-page illustrations in these earlier journals. Among the strangest is this naked, hairy man holding a sapling while he draws chalk crosses on a wall, beneath a pack of playing cards.

British Queen's engines, boiler and water weighed 500 tons, and that she would consume an estimated 600 tons of coal on a twenty-day voyage.

The Rock Ferry Company sought to raise £35,000, part of which would be directed towards the acquisition of new ferries such as the *Cheshire Witch*. The scheme found no shortage of investors, and services began shortly after.

The company's lawyer was to be busy in the next few years. The crossing between Rock Ferry and George's Pier represented a journey of about a mile along a crowded estuary barely 600 yards wide. Ferry masters regularly battled adverse tidal conditions, wind, fog and fading light as they strove to adhere to a demanding timetable. There were knocks and collisions between ferries, which were alarming and expensive to repair, but perhaps the greatest danger was to the smaller craft which were forced to share the river with these noisy, impatient contraptions.

On Friday 4 August 1843, Captain Samuel Lloyd guided the *Cheshire Witch* away from George's Pier and headed upriver on the evening crossing. He hugged the Liverpool shoreline somewhat, as steamer masters tended to do, to avoid the stronger current in the centre of the river. As the *Cheshire Witch* passed Coburg Dock, a small boat appeared in her path, in it a crew of two and ten passengers on their way to visit friends on a vessel at anchor.[5]

Lloyd tried to avoid the danger in front of him. He altered his course inshore but was forced outward again to avoid a pier. He gestured and shouted, but at that moment the little boat was helpless. Her boatmen had been in the process of hoisting her sails and had use of neither the sails nor oars, one of which was already at her stern as a rudder.

The *Cheshire Witch* struck before her paddles could be reversed. The small boat turned over and sank. Rescuers brought ten men to shore while an eleventh was saved by an onlooker who jumped off the pier and seized him as he sank. The body of the twelfth, William Johnson, was recovered a few days later. Captain Lloyd faced a charge of manslaughter but was acquitted, in part due to his active role in rescuing those thrown into the river.

The Rock Ferry Company was to have its ups and downs in the coming years and would go through several different owners, as each new consortium attempted to make a go of it. There were periods of profit, but also challenges, most notably the opening of the first Mersey tunnel in 1886. Ferry services from Rock Ferry finally ceased in 1939.

Regardless of the outcome of his investment, John Nelson Wood and his wife Mary found Rock Ferry to be an agreeable location. They made their home in Rock Park, and John Nelson continued to work as a broker, shipowner and alderman for many years, with a finger in many pies. He died in 1855, when his fortunes became fatefully entangled once more with those of the family shipyard.

Kelsick had shown that his yard could adjust to building wooden vessels suitable for steam engines, but other technical advances would prove harder to accommodate.

Among the most charming of Kelsick's drawings is this picture of a smartly dressed young boy playing with a dog. Kelsick's entries on the lower part of the page relate to the account of Ann Marshall, widow of Edward, the coach driver killed with Wilton when their horse took fright near Moresby Hall. The boy shown here may be Ann's son, John, who would have been about nine years old when this page was prepared.

THE *MARY* (1838): FROM IRON FIXINGS TO IRON HULLS

The dominance of the two-masted merchant brig was slowly fading, but commissions like the *Cheshire Witch* and the *Mary* show Kelsick pushing at the edges of what his yard could achieve.

The *Mary* was a three-masted ship, a relative rarity for Kelsick's yard and, at 694 tons burthen, she was twice the size of the yard's more typical build. She was the largest vessel built anywhere in Cumberland at the time.

Her launch in January 1838 came four years after the removal of the last of the mighty East India Company's trade monopolies with India and China. The Company's huge ships, which carried tea and other produce through the southern seas, would have dwarfed the brigs and sloops most commonly being built along the Cumberland coast, but these lucrative markets in the East Indies were now open to all-comers.

Her principal owner was Liverpool merchant John Ridgway, and he had commissioned her with exactly these markets in mind. The *Mary* sailed between London and the ports of Madras and Canton throughout the 1840s, apparently making good time on the route from London to Bombay, completing it in eighty-two days on her first sailing and later in just seventy-one days, 'the shortest passage on record'. Along with her greater cargo capacity, the *Mary* was also fitted out with berths for 'cabin, intermediate, and steerage passengers', a step up from those offered by a small brig like the *Stirlingshire*.[6]

The *Mary* spent much of 1842 contracted to the East India Company. Since the mid-eighteenth century, the Company had grown from trading organisation to India's de facto national ruler. Acting with the authority of the British Crown, it controlled a large private army of European and Indian troops, which it deployed to quell rebellions, for territorial gain and for defence of British interests in the region.

To the north-west, Afghanistan was seen as an important obstacle to Russian and Persian ambitions. Given India's significance to the empire, Britain made diplomatic approaches and then took military steps to ensure that the country would not form any unfavourable alliances. The conflict, the First Anglo-Afghan War, proved to be a humiliating disaster for the British, culminating in the chaotic retreat from Kabul in which over 16,000 lives were lost. It left the East India Company vulnerable and its local army depleted.

From its headquarters in London, the Company commissioned a flotilla of thirty-three merchant vessels to deliver much-needed reinforcements, the *Mary* among them. The *Morning Advertiser* reported on their departure in April 1842. Gravesend, it said, had recently exhibited the appearance of a garrison town, 'thousands of troops being in it'. Among them were a thousand men of the 78th Regiment of Highlanders, 'The Ross-shire Buffs', with the *Mary* selected to carry its officers and staff.

This was the last that many of these men would see of England. After their disembarkation at Bombay, the 78th Highlanders were stationed first at Poona before travelling to Karachi, with orders to march to the town of Sukkur, several hundred miles along the swampy banks of the River Indus. A virulent fever swept through the regiment shortly after they arrived at the town and left hundreds sick or dying from what was later identified as cholera. Captain Keogh of the regiment described the unfolding horror in bleak detail in his journal, 'Day after day we attended at the hospital for ... funeral parade; ... four or five, and then eight or nine, men died daily; you did not ask who had died, but how many.'[7]

With the fever initially attributed to malaria, the regiment was sent downriver to Hyderabad to escape the area's mosquitoes, but many more died during the hot, humid days and cold, damp nights aboard the fleet of small boats. Between September 1844 and April 1845, the 78th Highlanders lost more than 500 men and officers, and nearly 200 women and children, or, as Keogh put it, 'total 737 souls'.

The *Carlisle Journal*'s description of the *Mary* on her launch day highlights an aspect of late Georgian shipbuilding which is easily overlooked. These were wooden-hulled vessels with wooden masts, but metals were already being widely incorporated.

> In strength ... this splendid specimen of naval architecture excells any of the numerous first-rate vessels built in the same yard. She is copper-fastened and coppered to the bends; her timbers are of extraordinary dimensions, and the wrought iron used in her binding alone weighs nearly thirty tons!

In his 1948 book *The Shipwright's Trade*, Sir Westcott Abell imagines a conversation between a Georgian shipwright, a smithy and a boiler maker, naming them as Tom, Dick and Harry. The three men talk about the possibility of building a ship entirely from iron. One can build wooden ships, another can work with iron and the third, the boiler maker, is skilled in fabrication. Tom the shipwright starts with disbelief, 'It's flying against nature, that's what it is, since we all know that wood floats and iron sinks', but his hostility fades and the three men start to tackle the technical challenges, one by one. Each brings essential expertise, but no one man has the full set of knowledge required.

Abell is suitably generous in his portrayal of the shipwright. Tom is an intelligent man, puzzling over engineering problems posed by this unfamiliar material. Shipbuilders like Kelsick may have pondered the same engineering challenges, but not all had the skills, the space or the foresight to respond. Abell says that it should be no surprise that many of the first companies to build iron hulls were engine and boiler makers, where platers and riveters knew already how to cut, bend, shape and join sheets of metal.

Small, iron-hulled steamers first appeared in the 1820s, but problems needed to be overcome before the technology could be used for ocean-going vessels. The iron interfered with compass readings and an iron hull could not be sheathed directly with copper to prevent fouling, due to the corrosive reaction between the two

Registration documents can be a wonderful trove of information. The form asked for a description of the vessel's 'head'. We learn that the *Agnes Wood* carried a seahorse figurehead, the *Irishman* a woman and harp bust and the *Spaniel* a dog's figurehead. The *Coeur de Lion* carried a lion bust, shown here.

metals. Over time, though, these problems were solved and iron found its way to the heart of the shipbuilding process.

The shape of ships changed as a result. Sides grew straighter and the reduction in the bulk of the internal frame increased cargo capacity. The change in materials allowed larger ships to be built, capable of carrying more powerful engines. A new breed of mechanised shipyards appeared, at Birkenhead to the south, Glasgow to the north and around the Tyne and Wear rivers on the east coast. Kelsick Wood & Sons, its ambitions constrained by the width of North Harbour and the houses and hills behind it, had neither the space nor the resources to compete.

The final ship that Isambard Kingdom Brunel built, the SS *Great Eastern*, was launched in 1858. Brunel's new creation showcased many of the innovations which hailed the downfall of Maryport's original shipyard. The *Great Eastern* was steam-powered, iron-hulled and fitted with both screw propeller and side paddles, and she was enormous, 692 feet from bow to stern, several times the length of the entire Kelsick Wood & Sons shipbuilding yard.

Chapter 5
Decline

Man wants the skill, and earth the dyes,
To light the sun and paint the skies.
'The Setting Sun' (extract)

Jonathan Douglas's health is failing as he walks along Maryport's shoreline and admires the colours of the evening sky. As the sun sinks low towards the horizon, he sees his own short life reflected in its path.

The tranquil delight of watching a West Cumberland sunset is a pleasure on which William Russell also dwells as he brings his speech to a close. Their two contributions, from the 1830s and the 1890s, neatly bookend the changing world of Queen Victoria's long reign, a world in which small, provincial builders of wooden sailing ships finally found that they had no place.

To tie the end of the Age of Sail to a specific event is inevitably to invite disagreement. It was a slow diminishing, a gradual loss of relevance, rather than a sudden moment of collapse. There were markers along the way, particular innovations and engineering feats to be lauded and the arrival of landmark vessels such as the *Great Eastern*. Those of a naval bent might state the Battle of Navarino in 1827 as the key moment, the last battle fought solely between sailing vessels. Someone with a merchant focus might put the date much later.

The rise of sleek tea clippers brought about a short-lived resurgence in the prestige of sail between the 1840s and 1860s. Famous clippers like the *Taeping* and *Ariel* captured the British public's imagination as they raced to deliver the first of the new season's Chinese tea to London's auction houses. Tea clippers were the greyhounds of nineteenth-century sailing ships, sleek, streamlined and designed for speed. Their composite hulls united the best of the old and the new: an interior iron framework to maximise storage capacity, and exterior wood planking, which allowed the hull to be sheathed in copper.

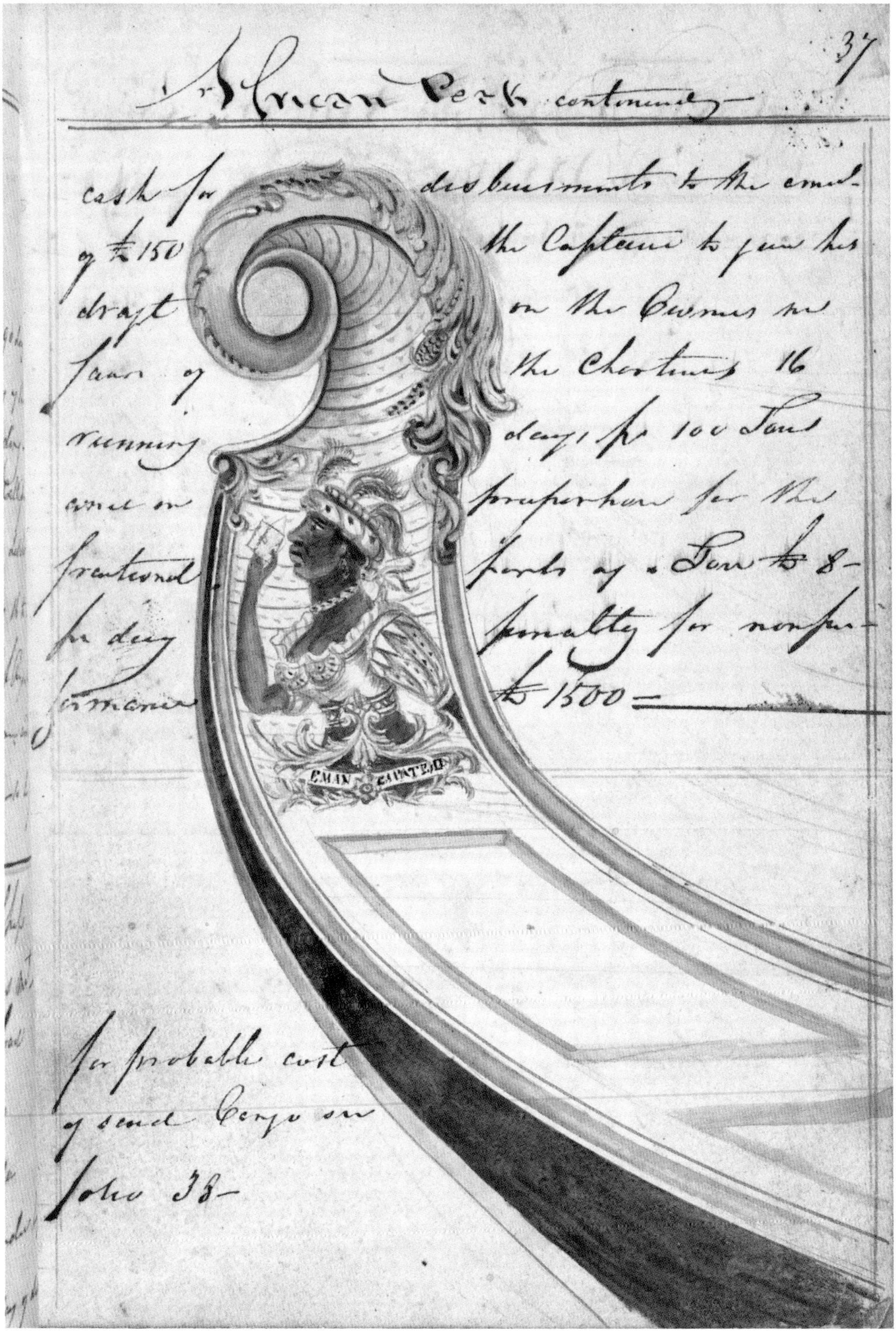

Note the 'Emancipation' scroll at the lady's waist on this trailboard design, another celebration of 1833's Slavery Abolition Act.

Despite their general magnificence, the clippers' celebrity tailed off after the opening of the Suez Canal in 1869. The 120-mile waterway between the Mediterranean and the Red Sea shortened journeys to India and Asia by 3,000 nautical miles but highlighted one of sail's basic limitations. The region's prevailing wind is from the north. While homebound steamships could return northwards to Europe via the canal, sailing ships had no room to tack within the narrow channel and could only take the longer, slower route around the Cape of Good Hope. Some clippers were repurposed for less glamorous roles. The *Cutty Sark*, now raised high in its dry dock in Greenwich, was used to carry wool from Australia to England between 1883 and 1895, until improvements to steam technology meant that too became uneconomical.

Sailing vessels remained important to the Cumberland coal industry well into the 1880s. Unlike high-value tea, where freshness could command a premium, coal was a bulky, low-margin cargo and speed of delivery was of less importance. On top of that, many of the smaller destination ports around the Irish and Scottish coastline lacked much infrastructure. A sturdy coal brig could sit on the sand at Dumfries or Wigtown for a week or two being unloaded manually at low tide, with little impact on the operator's bottom line. Although orders for new vessels became increasingly rare, the need to maintain these older coastal brigs held up for longer.[1]

Kelsick did not live to see these developments. He died from liver disease in 1840, aged sixty-eight, three years after the launch of the *Cheshire Witch*. The *Carlisle Journal* focused its long obituary on his character and compassion:

> To all the charitable institutions of his native town, Mr Wood was a liberal contributor; and when ever an effort was made to aid any unfortunate family, or bereaved widow, by a private subscription, he was sure to be found at the head of the list. Mr Wood was one in whom all nature might stand up and say – 'here is a man'.

Just as the Wood family had done before, the next generation of shipbuilders picked up where Kelsick had left off. John Wood, who had worked alongside his father since the 1820s, took over the business, in partnership with his brother, Kelsick Junior. The brothers kept their father's name above the door and continued to build the vessels for which he had been so renowned, but the challenges which Kelsick had confronted grew only more acute for those who followed him. As the weavers and spinners of the textile industry had learnt several decades earlier, the glory days for small, manual enterprises had passed.[2]

By the end of the 1840s, the yard's fortunes were waning. In 1849, John arranged a loan of £8,000 from Head's Bank in Carlisle to prop up the business, secured against the assets of his half-brother, John Nelson, an act of familial duty which John Nelson would come to regret.

The yard's financial situation continued to worsen. John and Kelsick Junior dissolved their partnerships and attempted to separate their interests. Kelsick Junior took control of their sailmaking business, and John was left with sole responsibility for the mounting debts of the shipyard.

John slid slowly towards bankruptcy and began to sell off property and other assets to meet his obligations. A local auctioneer announced the sale of John's portfolio of ship shares in October 1852, followed by a second sale in April 1853. Twelve years had passed since Kelsick's death and most of the vessels listed were more recent creations, but the *Wilton Wood* (2/64ths) remained among them.

These sales provided temporary relief, but the problems ran too deep. The entire shipyard was put up for sale in 1853, to be sold at auction at the Golden Lion on 16 June, where the 'old and well-known firm of Kelsick Wood and Sons' was offered for sale as a single lot, comprising timber, yards, moulding and rigging lofts, smithy and offices, together with an obligation to purchase the metal patent slip, stove and boiler. There would also be the opportunity to buy the chattels connected with the yard, everything from the carpenters' tools to the smithy's bellows. It was advertised as 'worthy the attention of Capitalists, or a Joint Stock Company desirous of embarking extensively into the Business of Building and Repairing Ships', but interest appears to have been muted.

The following year, Head's Bank demanded repayment of its £8,000 loan. When John was unable to pay, the bank turned to the guarantor, John Nelson, who watched in horror as the scale of his liability was revealed and as his own personal fortune came tumbling down.

The yard remained in John Wood's hands at the end of this period of turmoil, either as tenant or owner. He renamed it to John Wood & Co. and shifted his focus more fully onto repair work. Cumberland's newspapers still reported on an occasional new vessel, a schooner in 1857 with a second vessel to be launched the following spring, but mentions were less frequent and without the old fanfare.

On John's death in 1859, his son Wilton William became the fourth generation of Woods to run Maryport's oldest shipyard. The young Wilton rose to the challenge as best he could. He invested in a new patent slip, announcing proudly that the yard would be able to haul larger vessels out of the water for repair, and built what proved to be the yard's final vessel, a brigantine named the *Flimby*, launched in July 1862. These stories receive attention from local newspapers but, as the decade passes, the mentions slowly come to an end. A local youth named Hugh McGarry is charged in 1867 with tearing down a railing outside the yard for use as firewood, but there is little else. Maryport's oldest shipyard has faded quietly into history.

Five decades after the yard's closure, a surveyor visited the town in 1911 and picked through the remains of what had once been Kelsick Wood & Sons.[3] The decline which had befallen the Wood family business had echoed across much of the community. The town's other shipyards had closed or were closing. The last to shut its gates was Ritson's, which had thrived and then survived under various names and owners until about the time of the surveyor's report. As demand for new vessels had changed, the Ritson family had sought to change with it, building hulls with wood, iron and later steel, and for sail or steam as the project dictated (although each new steam vessel had to be towed to the Clyde for its engine to be fitted). The yard continued to draw crowds for its dramatic, broadside launches, but ultimately it could not compete with the new generation of shipbuilding centres around Britain's coast and beyond.

I came across the survey late in the preparation of this book and it made for surprisingly emotional reading, despite its dry tone and endless measurements and notes on properties. The surveyor was visiting a town in decline, with rising unemployment, little investment and limited prospects. The volume of coal exports was falling and many of the town's other industries had departed. I had lived with Kelsick Wood, his journals and the stories of his yard for several years, and it was saddening to see that, already by 1911, only faint, dusty echoes could be found of the business which had once sent forth its wooden ships to all corners of the world.

The shipbuilding yard next to North Harbour had been derelict for many years and was being used chiefly as a poultry run, with a small tallow factory in one corner. The buildings arranged around the boat yard were still standing, but now in a poor state of repair and stripped of signs of their original purpose. The house on Strand Street, home to generations of the Wood family, had been reconfigured for multiple occupancy. The surveyor noted dispassionately, 'This is a fairly good property – appears to have been a large house at one time.'

Today, signs of the yard's existence are even harder to find. The site where the busy shipyard once operated, where Kelsick sat in his office with his ink pen and his watercolours, and where a century of nameless shipwrights crafted their brigs and ships, is now grassland opposite a line of seafront houses, put up in the 1960s. A 6-foot flood wall, painted with the protest message 'No Flats', splits the site, separating the shoreline from the houses behind.

Not everything is lost. North Harbour remains, the same waves still beating against North Pier's same sturdy defences. The little iron lighthouse stands opposite, and there also remains a strong pride in the town's maritime heritage. A short walk from North Harbour stands Maryport's Maritime Museum. Among its collection is another of Kelsick's journals, ready once more to cast its spell on those who open it.

Epilogue

In May 1839, as Kelsick entered his final year, J. M. W. Turner's *The Fighting Temeraire* was hanging in the East Room of the Royal Academy on London's Piccadilly. It was met with critical ambivalence at the time but is now recognised as one of the most poignant insights into this era. Turner paints the ninety-eight-gun HMS *Temeraire*, one of the hero ships of the Battle of Trafalgar, as she is towed up the Thames to be broken up for scrap at Rotherhithe.

The sun is setting and the pale, ghostly shape of the *Temeraire* is no longer fighting. Stripped of her sails and her seamen, the once-glorious man-of-war is led to her fate by a small paddle-wheel steam tug, its chimney belching fire and dirty smoke back towards the old wooden ship. Whether Turner intends us to view the steam-powered tug as dark and ominous or as a worthy successor to the mighty sailing ships that have come before, one thing is certain: the world is changing.[1]

The Fighting Temeraire, tugged to her last berth to be broken up, 1838, Joseph Mallord William Turner. (© The National Gallery, London. All rights reserved)

Acknowledgements

I have built a deep affection for the little town of Maryport during the preparation of this book. Its nineteenth-century glory days may be behind it, but I wish the town and all its residents a bright future.

The writing of this book has only been possible because of the support offered by so many people along the way, among them the following. Sincere apologies to anyone I have missed. Alison and the team at Amberley. Emma Donovan and Martyn Beardsley for guidance and encouragement. David Malcolm for insights and friendship. David Atkinson of Hand Made Maps. Luca Rapisarda at the Lloyd's Register Foundation. Sarah Lee, Bryan Mawer and Len Barnett. John and Ann Ferguson for genealogical information on the Wood family. Ray Greenhow for insights into John Kent. Ian Smith. David Bridgwater. Thanks also to Jeremy Michell, curator at Royal Museums Greenwich, and the teams at The National Archives and the Cumbria Archive Service. And thanks always to Karine, my wife and best friend.

Notes

1. ORIGINS

1. Maryport Harbour Act 1748 (22 Geo. 2. c. 6) (Royal assent: 22 March 1749).
2. Wood letters: Ferguson, *Archive of the Wood Family, Vol. I* (Cold Harbour Press, 2024).

2. AROUND THE YARD

1. Yard description sources: *Carlisle Patriot*, 11 June 1853; Whitehaven Archive DWM 279/228.
2. Kelsick's carved bust: Winterthur Museum, Delaware (1968.0018).
3. Navigation Acts: *Essays in Economic History, Vol. III* (Arnold, 1962), J. H. Clapham, 'The Last Years of the Navigation Acts'; *Accounts and Papers of the House of Commons, Vol. 18* (1827), 'Petition of the Ship Owners of the Port of London, 1823'.
4. Sanitation: *Mr John Spear's Report … on the prevalence of 'Fever' in … Maryport* (E&S for HMSO, 1882).
5. Lloyd's Register: *Journal of the Society of Arts*, 6 May 1859, 337/VII (RSA, 1859), p. 428; J. R. McCulloch, *A Dictionary … of Commerce and Commercial Navigation* (Longman, 1835).
6. *Campbell*: Survey report 12 Jan. 1837 (LR Foundation); LR General Committee minute book, 1837.
7. Figureheads: E. McCarthy, 'Ship Carvers in 18th and 19th Century Britain', *Sculpture Journal*, 24.2 (LUP, 2015); D. I. Smith, 'James and George Brooker: West Cumberland shipcarvers …' (CWAAS, 2000).
8. Sail and cordage approximations are based on the replica brig *Lady Washington* (launched in the US, 1989).
9. Unrest: *Star (London)*, 26 October 1825; *Cumberland Pacquet*, 25 October 1825, 1 November 1825, 7 March 1826; *Trades' Free Press*, 30 April 1826.
10. *Collingwood*'s launch: *Cumberland Pacquet*, 9 December 1828; William Mitchell's painting reproduced with kind permission of Bonhams.

3. ONCE AT SEA

1. Quote from A CUMBRIAN: *Liverpool Albion*, 13 August 1827.
2. Senhouse's birthday dinner: *Cumberland Pacquet*, 2 December 1834.
3. *Eliza Heywood* principal source: Whitehaven Archive DH/56; Also, *Hampshire Independent*, 1 June 1872.
4. *Frances Watson*: TNA: HCA 1/110; *Sun (London)*, 2 July 1829; *Morning Post*, 16 July 1829; *Cumberland Pacquet*, 7 July 1829.
5. Bragg's murder: *Launceston Advertiser*, 31 December 1835; Sarah Lee, 'Surprising Seafarers', *Family Tree Magazine* (2016).
6. *Agnes Wood*: *Welshman*, 30 December 1836; *Carlisle Patriot*, 21 January 1837.
7. *Nelson Wood*: *Cumberland Pacquet*, 12 December 1843; *Carlisle Journal* (quoting *The Times*), 16 December 1843; *Shipping and Mercantile Gazette*, 13 December 1843.
8. Maryport Harbour and Improvement Act 1833 (3 & 4 Will. 4. c. cxiii) (viewed at Carlisle Archive, DCR 20).
9. *Campbell*'s launch: *Cumberland Pacquet*, 17 January 1837.
10. Launches: *Martha: Carlisle Journal*, 22 December 1838; *Lord Ellenborough: Carlisle Patriot*, 24 January 1824; *Princess Charlotte: Evening Mail*, 19 September 1825; *Daphne: Dundee Courier*, 13 July 1883; *Albion: Illustrated Police News*, 2 July 1898; *Dowthorpe: Suffolk Chronicle*, 22 July 1854.
11. George Dawson's will: Carlisle Archive, DLAW/1/75.
12. Dawson's sugar sales: J. Holmes, *Law Journal Reports for 1858, Vol. 27* (Ince, 1858); N. Deerr, *The History of Sugar, Vol. II* (C&H, 1949).
13. Downfall: *Cumberland Pacquet*, 14 January 1845; *Lyttelton Times*, 22 January 1859; *Whitehaven News*, 21 October 1858; *The Law Times Reports, Vol. XXXVI* (Cox) 'Dawson vs Bank of Whitehaven'; N. C. Moak, *Reports of Cases Decided by the English Courts, Vol. XX* (Gould, 1879).
14. Slavery in British Guiana: R. T. Smith, *The Negro Family in British Guiana* (Routledge, 1956), Ch. III.
15. John Bolton: D. Pope, 'Bolton, John (1756–1837)', Oxford Dictionary of National Biography, 2016.
16. Rescue: *Belfast News-Letter*, 19 September 1837; *Morning Herald*, 16 September 1837; *Sun (London)*, 14 December 1837; *Newry Telegraph*, 19 September 1837.
17. Sale adverts: *Liverpool Standard*, 20 October 1837; *Liverpool Mercury*, 15 December 1837.
18. S. F. Brown, *Bonaparte & Brimstone* (The Conrad Press, 2023).
19. *Donegall*: *Carlisle Patriot*, 2 March 1833.
20. Matches 1823 voyage: *Inverness Journal*, 9 January 1824.
21. Scollay in Sydney: *Sydney Gazette*, 10 September 1836, 8 November 1836.
22. Robert Russell: *Australian Dictionary of Biography, Vol. II* (MUP, 1967) H. Preston article; *La Trobeana*, 16.2 (2017). F. Woodhouse article 'Politics, Power and Passion: Port Phillip before the gold rush'.

23. Maria Monro: *New Zealand Scrapbook, Feb.–Nov. 1958* (APL).
24. *Widow's Friend*: *Cumberland Pacquet*, 25 September 1832; *Lancaster Gazette*, 17 November 1832; *Caernarvon & Denbigh Herald*, 11 January 1834; *Register of Shipping for the Year 1833* (Marchant, 1833).
25. *Thomas Parsons*: *Liverpool Mercantile Gazette*, 20 July 1835; *Liverpool Albion*, 1 August 1836, 17 February 1834; *Chester Courant*, 9 June 1840.
26. *Black Prince*: *Lloyd's List*, 25 May 1984, D. Burrell 'Shedding Light on Yesteryear's Ocean Wanderers'.
27. *James Ray*: *Morning Herald*, 30 March 1852.
28. *Bella Portena*: *Barbadian*, 18 July to 12 August 1857.
29. *Irishman*: D. Ramshaw, *The Carlisle Ship Canal 1821–1853* (P3 Publications, 2013).

4. CHALLENGES

1. Smith A., *An Inquiry into the Nature and Causes of The Wealth of Nations, Vol. II* (Legrand, 1791).
2. Wilton's speech: *Cumberland Pacquet*, 2 February 1830; *Devizes & Wiltshire Gazette*, 14 July 1825; *Morning Chronicle*, 30 January 1830; A. and W. Wood, *A Selection of Scraps* (1832).
3. Wilton's accident: *Cumberland Pacquet*, 8 May 1832; *Public Ledger*, 11 May 1832.
4. Royal Rock Ferry Steam Packet Co.: *Liverpool Standard*, 1 April 1836; *Liverpool Albion*, 30 April 1838.
5. *Cheshire Witch* collision: *Liverpool Mail*, 12 August 1843, 2 September 1843.
6. *Mary* sources: *Cumberland Pacquet*, 30 October 1838; *Morning Advertiser*, 20 April 1842.
7. 78th Highlanders: J. S. Keltie (ed.), *History of the Scottish Highlands* (Mackenzie, London), Vol. II.

5. DECLINE

1. D. Clarke, *Coastwise from Cumberland: Maryport Coastal Trade, 1855–1889* (thesis) (MUN, 1997).
2. Yard's decline: *Carlisle Journal*, 23 May 1840; *Maryport Advertiser*, 1 August 1862; *Liverpool Journal of Commerce*, 24 June 1863; *Whitehaven News*, 21 November 1867; Whitehaven Archive DWM 279/228; Carlisle Archive DRIC/74.
3. 1911 survey: TNA: IR 135/1/875, IR 58/19213, IR 58/189215.

EPILOGUE

1. Turner: *The Exhibition of the Royal Academy, MDCCCXXXIX* (Clowes, 1839).

Select Bibliography

PRIMARY SOURCES

Journals of Kelsick Wood (volumes numbered 2, 3 and 4) (private collection)
Journal and sketchbook of Kelsick Wood (Caird Library SPB/45/1-2)
Journal of Kelsick Wood (volume numbered 6) (Maryport Maritime Museum)
William Russell, 'Maryport in 1832', Public Lecture at the Old Court House, 1896 (Carlisle Archive DCR/1)
Maryport Harbour and Shipping (Whitehaven Archive DCR/20-25)
Eliza Heywood, brig, of Whitehaven (Whitehaven Archive DH/56)
The ship building yard of Kelsick Wood and Sons at Maryport (Whitehaven Archive DWM/279/228)
Registry of Shipping and Seamen: Transcripts and Transactions, Series I (The National Archives BT107)

BOOKS

Abell, Sir W., *The Shipwright's Trade* (Cambridge: CUP, 1948)
Ashmore, B. G., *Maryport Harbour, A Short History and Description* (Workington: CN Print, 1978)
Ayton, R., *A Voyage Round Great Britain, Vol. II* (London: Longman, 1815)
Doe, H., *Enterprising Women and Shipping in the Nineteenth Century* (Woodbridge: Boydell Press, 2009)
Douglas, J., *Miscellaneous Poems* (Maryport: 1836)
Ferguson, J. and A., *Captain Kelsick Wood (1771–1840)* (Wooler: Cold Harbour Press, 2021)
Fincham, J., *An Introductory Outline of the Practice of Ship-Building &c &c.* (Portsea: Woodward, 1821)
Forsyth, A., *Highway to the World* (Carlisle: Bookcase, 2011)

Greenhow, R., *Britain's First Black Policeman* (Carlisle: Bookcase, 2018)
Jackson, H. and M., *Seagoing West Cumbrians* (Maryport: Hirst-Jackson, 1995)
Robinson, A., *Maryport's Great Shipbuilding Yards & Ships* (Workington: CN Print, n.d.)
Stammers, M., 'Slipways and steamchests', *IJNA*, Vol. 28, Issue 3, August 1999
Wells, J. D., *Maritime Maryport* (Kendal: Wilson, 2012)
Wells, J. D., *Maryport, The Passing Years* (Kendal: Wilson, 2006)
Wood, A. and W., *A Selection of Scraps in Prose and Verse* (Liverpool: Groom, 1832)

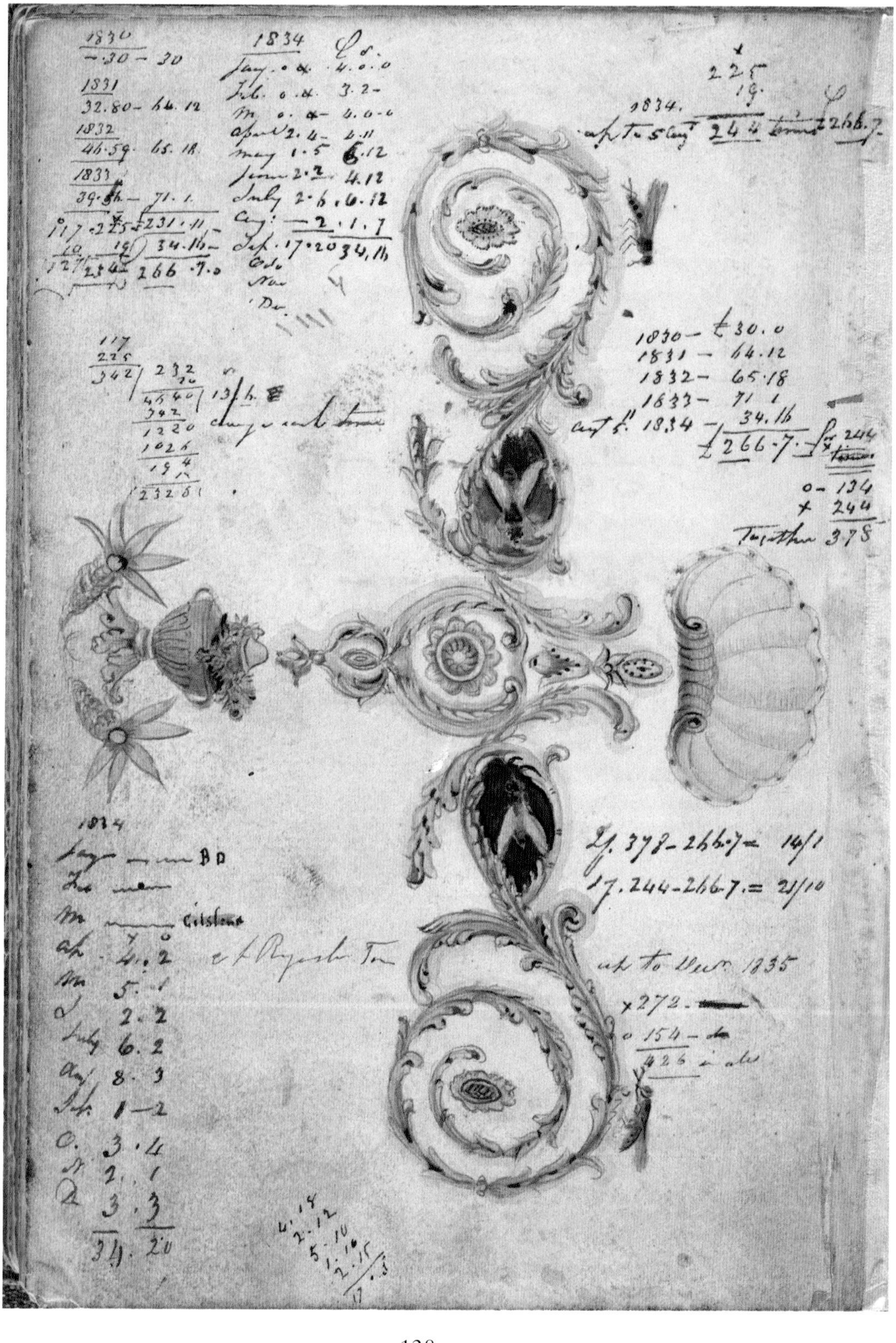

1830 – £30.0
1831 – 64.12
1832 – 65.18
1833 – 71 1
1834 – 34.16
£266.7.